THE BIBLE—YOU CAN BELIEVE IT

Biblical Authority in the Twenty-First Century

A BAPTIST DOCTRINE AND HERITAGE STUDY FOR LIFE TODAY

James C. Denison

BAPTISTWAYPRESS®
Dallas, Texas

BAPTISTWAY PRESS® Management Team
Executive Director, Baptist General Convention of Texas: Charles Wade
Director, Missions, Evangelism, and Ministry Team: Wayne Shuffield
Director, Bible Study/Discipleship Center: Dennis Parrott

Editor & publishing consultant: Ross West, Positive Difference Communications
Cover and Interior Design and Production: Desktop Miracles, Inc.

This book is produced in cooperation with the Baptist Distinctives Committee/Texas Baptist Heritage Center of the Baptist General Convention of Texas—Executive Director Emeritus, BGCT, and volunteer Director, Texas Baptist Heritage Center, William M. Pinson, Jr.; Chair of Baptist Distinctives Committee, James Semple.

First edition: November 2005
ISBN: 1-931060-71-1

The Bible—You Can Believe It

About This Doctrine, Heritage, and Life Study

This book is one of a series of books on Baptist doctrine and heritage that BAPTISTWAY PRESS® is producing annually. These studies are intended both for individual reading and study and for group studies in churches and other settings.

The intent of this series is to provide guidance in considering, understanding, and acting on some of our deeply-held Baptist beliefs, particularly as these beliefs intersect with current life. The intent is *not* to produce an official statement about these Baptist beliefs. Even to attempt to do so would go against the very nature of who Baptists are.

So, as you read and study this book and the other studies in the series, be prepared to think seriously and carefully. Engage the ideas with your own thought and study, especially of the Bible.

In addition to this study book, suggestions for teaching this study are available in *The Bible—You Can Believe It: Teaching Guide*. See www.baptistwaypress.org for additional resources for this and other studies produced by BAPTISTWAY PRESS®.

The Writer

James C. Denison, the author of *The Bible—You Can Believe It*, is pastor of Park Cities Baptist Church, Dallas, Texas. Other pastorates include Second-Ponce de Leon Baptist Church, Atlanta, Georgia, and First Baptist Church, Midland, Texas. Dr. Denison has also taught Philosophy of Religion at Southwestern Baptist Theological Seminary. He is a graduate of Houston Baptist University and Southwestern Seminary (M.Div., Ph.D.).

Introduction

The Tsunami in Biblical Authority

YOU AND I ARE LIVING in an age unlike any in American history. It's as though the North Pole has been removed from the globe and our compasses no longer work. Our churches and denominations are as confused as we are.

Baptists in America came of age in an era of objective truth and accepted moral standards. In the 1950s, Baptists' greatest decade of numerical growth and expansion, when Ward Cleaver came home from work, his family sat down to dinner together—Ward in his suit and June in her dress and pearls, while Wally and the Beaver ate quietly and respectfully. Although they didn't know it, the Cleavers were the last stop on the road to a changing world.

It would not be long before the Vietnam War divided the nation, the sexual revolution and drug culture made the news each night, and commitment to objective values was attacked from all sides. In fact, the cultural earthquakes of the 1960s are still shaking the foundations of our churches today, with no end in sight.

Now for the first time in history, three different worldviews are trying to sit in the same pew on Sunday morning. The World War II generation remembers a day when parents were in charge and biblical authority was unquestioned. Their children are the legacy of the 60s and its rejection of objective truth and values, including those of Scripture. Their grandchildren are heirs of the technological revolution, less interested in biblical "truth" but fascinated with "spirituality." How did the world change so much, so quickly?

These cataclysmic shifts in our culture did not occur in a vacuum. The tsunami that struck Southeast Asia on December 26, 2004, came without warning, but the tsunami that is shaking our churches and denominations was a long time in arriving on our shores. What earthquakes started the tidal waves? What are we to do about them? How can Baptists explain and defend our commitment to biblical authority in this new century? Why should we? Such questions and their answers are what this study is about.

CHAPTER One
The Bible Is God's Book

What Baptists Believe About Biblical Authority

New Hope Baptist Church was founded in the rural countryside of Texas in 1885. Located somewhat adjacent to Fort Worth but closer to Mansfield, the church began meeting in the country school that gave the congregation its name. One of the founding families donated land across Dick Price Road from the schoolhouse, and the church built its first sanctuary several generations ago. It constructed its last building in 1971, a structure some older members still call the "new sanctuary."

Times have changed around New Hope. The area has skyrocketed in growth. The cities of Fort Worth, Arlington, and Mansfield have marched ever closer to the church's property. The more the culture changes, however, the more many church members want their congregation to remain the same. It is an island of tranquility in a sea of chaos. In fact, that is its attraction and value to many of its people.

I started my pastoral ministry when New Hope called me to serve as pastor. Our two sons were born while we lived in the church parsonage, a yellow cottage adjacent to the church parking lot. Some of the deepest friendships I have ever known remain from those years. I have never experienced a more loving family of faith.

But I nearly didn't become the church's pastor. On the Sunday evening after I had preached "in view of a call" and received a wonderful vote from the congregation, the pulpit committee chairman called me at home. He and the committee had forgotten to mention a problem. The church constitution specified that the pastor must preach from the King James Version of the Bible. I had not done so that day (since I didn't own a KJV translation). Would I be willing to change? If not, the call would have to be rescinded. That week my wife bought me a black leather King James Version Bible, and our ministry began.

For New Hope Baptist Church, the one foundation that had stood solid across more than a century of change was the Bible. Pastors and staff had come and gone; programs and property had changed; but the congregation was committed to the truth of God's word. This was the one priority without which the church would lose its way.

I'm now in my fourth decade of Baptist life and ministry. I have been privileged to teach and preach as part of Baptist work on five continents. The one commonality I have found in every Baptist church and every Baptist ministry, from California to Georgia to East Malaysia, from country churches to city congregations, from rural Bible studies to seminary classrooms, has been our commitment to biblical authority.

Why do Baptists believe the Bible? What exactly do we believe about it? Have our beliefs changed over the generations?

The larger subject of Baptists and the Bible is a topic of far greater history and detail than this book is intended to discuss. For our purposes, we'll focus on the major beliefs about Scripture that Baptists have articulated through their various statements of faith. Then we'll learn why these commitments still matter today.

The Nature of God's Word

The 1963 *Baptist Faith and Message* begins with this article about the Scriptures:

> *The Holy Bible was written by men divinely inspired and is the record of God's revelation of Himself to man. It is a perfect treasure of divine instruction. It has God for its author, salvation for its end, and truth, without any mixture of error, for its matter. It reveals the principles by which God judges us; and therefore is, and will remain to the end of the world, the true center of Christian union, and the supreme standard by which all human conduct, creeds, and religious opinions should be tried. The criterion by which the Bible is to be interpreted is Jesus Christ.*[1]

As we will discover shortly, the *Baptist Faith and Message* (abbreviated as BF&M)[2] was not intended to speak for all Baptists, or to prescribe personal belief. Rather, it is a compendium of what most Baptists have believed through our history on various subjects. Its description of the Bible is a succinct overview of these beliefs. Consider each of its phrases in turn.

The Bible was "written by men divinely inspired." Baptists believe in biblical inspiration, in the conviction that the Scriptures come from God. The BF&M does not specify a particular theory of inspiration. Some Baptists believe that God dictated the very words of Scripture to its writers. Others think that God gave them ideas, which they expressed using their own vocabularies. Others believe that God's word is the product of a divine/human partnership that the Holy Spirit protected and led. Baptists have never prescribed a particular approach to this question. But we have always believed that the Bible comes from God.

Scripture is "the record of God's revelation of Himself to man. It is a perfect treasure of divine instruction." God has revealed himself to us and has recorded this self-revelation in Scripture. The Bible is thus "perfect"; the word translated "perfect" in Scripture means *to be complete or entire, to accomplish its intended purpose* (see Matthew 5:48).[3] Its instructions are "divine," not human.

The Bible has "salvation for its end." It is a means to the end of personal faith in Christ. As John wrote in summarizing his Gospel, "these are written that you may believe that Jesus is the Christ, the Son of God, and that by believing you may have life in his name"

(John 20:31). We are not saved by trusting the Bible, but by trusting the God that Scripture reveals. Baptists read the Bible evangelistically.

The Bible is "truth, without any mixture of error, for its matter." This phrase, "without any mixture of error," goes back to the New Hampshire confession of 1833 and was included in the 1925 BF&M as well. It does not prescribe a particular definition or theory of inerrancy (see chapter ten of this book), but clearly affirms that the Bible is trustworthy and authoritative.

God's word is the "true center of Christian union," calling Baptists to unity without uniformity. We are united in the clear teachings of Scripture, not the various interpretations and convictions of men and women. We are not a creedal people. Rather, we find our unity only in divine revelation. Indeed, we believe that Scripture is "the supreme standard by which all human conduct, creeds, and religious opinions should be tried." We want to be like the Bereans, who "examined the Scriptures every day to see if what Paul said was true" (Acts 17:11).

Finally, "the criterion by which the Bible is to be interpreted is Jesus Christ." This crucial phrase means that we interpret all of God's written word in light of God's living Word (John 1:1, 14). Jesus is the "Lamb that was slain from the creation of the world" (Revelation 13:8). God's plan before time began was to bring his Son to save the world (John 3:16). All Scripture, from Genesis to Revelation, concerns this salvation strategy and its implications for our lives.

The Bible was not intended to discuss every dimension of knowledge and interest, but those issues that affect our relationship with our Father. Scripture is not written as a book of science, history, or logic. Rather, it is the means by which our Creator has revealed himself to his creation, so that we might be restored to relationship with him.

As a result, we are to ask of every passage in Scripture: *How does this reveal God in Christ? What does this text tell us about our relationship with our Redeemer?* Based on this revelation, what can I know about myself and my Father?

So Baptists believe that the Bible is the divinely inspired self-revelation of God to us, truth without mixture of error, calling us to salvation and union in Christ. Most Christians would agree with these affirmations. Are there convictions regarding biblical authority that are more distinctively Baptist?

What Baptists Distinctively Believe

Baptist historian Walter Shurden has articulated succinctly the "four fragile freedoms" Baptists embrace: Bible freedom, soul freedom, church freedom, and religious freedom. He states that we are free *under* the Lordship of Jesus Christ, and we insist on freedom of biblical interpretation because the Scriptures are the way we each come to Christ. We insist on freedom of access to the Bible *for* the purpose of developing a living faith in continuing obedience to God's revelation. We want to be free *from* all other religious authorities but Scripture. Too, we stand for freedom *of* interpretation, as we study God's word under the guidance of his Spirit.[4]

In other words, Baptists believe that we are each free to interpret the Scriptures for ourselves. However, we must interpret the Bible under the Lordship of Jesus, for the purpose of obeying God, free from human control or authority, but guided by the Holy Spirit. When we understand and study God's word in these ways, we approach God's word as Baptists.

This position leads to the following practical conclusions.

Creedalism

A very significant issue regarding biblical authority is creedalism, approaching the Bible through the authority of church and tradition (see chapter two). Baptists have stood throughout our history for the conviction, "no creed but Scripture."

When people join my church from other denominations, they often ask to see our creed. I show them a Bible. A confused look crosses their face, and I explain that Baptists have no statement of faith they must sign. We do not recite the Apostles' Creed or the Nicene Creed in worship. We do not insist on the Westminster

Confession of Faith as basic to our theology. We consider all creeds made by human beings to be secondary to biblical authority.

What about our own confessions of faith? The preamble to the 1963 BF&M sets out the view the authors of the BF&M took of their statements:

> (1) *That they constitute a consensus of opinion of some Baptist body, large or small, for the general instruction and guidance of our own people and others concerning those articles of the Christian faith which are most surely held among us. They are not intended to add anything to the simple conditions of salvation revealed in the New Testament, viz., repentance towards God and faith in Jesus Christ as Savior and Lord.*
>
> (2) *That we do not regard them as complete statements of our faith, having any quality of finality or infallibility. As in the past so in the future Baptists should hold themselves free to revise their statements of faith as may seem to them wise and expedient at any time.*
>
> (3) *That any group of Baptists, large or small have the inherent right to draw up for themselves and publish to the world a confession of their faith whenever they may think it advisable to do so.*
>
> (4) *That the sole authority for faith and practice among Baptists is the Scriptures of the Old and New Testaments. Confessions are only guides in interpretation, having no authority over the conscience.*
>
> (5) *That they are statements of religious convictions, drawn from the Scriptures, and are not to be used to hamper freedom of thought or investigation in other realms of life.*[5]

To summarize: the *Baptist Faith and Message* does not add conditions to salvation, state unchangeable theology, or limit interpretation or conscience. Clearly, "the sole authority for faith and practice among Baptists is the Scriptures." We don't sign anyone's faith statement, not even our own.

When I joined the faculty of Southwestern Baptist Theological Seminary in 1987, I was surprised to learn that I would be required to sign the 1963 BF&M, and to agree to teach "according and not contrary to" its teachings. Knowing our historical aversion to creeds, I was surprised by this requirement. The administrator with whom

I spoke explained the requirement this way: sign the document, but interpret it according to your convictions. That was a good Baptist decision.

Back in 1911, historian W. J. McGlothlin made clear our relation to creeds and confessions:

> *Being congregational and democratic in church government, Baptists have naturally been very free in making, changing, and using Confessions. There has never been among them any ecclesiastical authority which could impose a Confession upon their churches or other bodies. Their Confessions are, strictly speaking, statements of what a certain group of Baptists, large or small, did believe at a given time, rather than a creed which any Baptist must believe at all times in order to hold ecclesiastical position or to be considered a Baptist. In the latter sense there has been no Baptist creed.*[6]

Indeed, the *Baptist Faith and Message* is more properly titled "A Statement of the Baptist Faith and Message."[7] It is not *the* statement or a creed we must believe. Jesus claimed, "all authority in heaven and on earth has been given to me" (Matthew 28:18). If Jesus has *all* authority, then we have none. Baptists believe in no creed but Scripture.

To be interpreted personally

W. B. Johnson was the first president of the Southern Baptist Convention. In 1846 he published a book that opposed confessions of faith as a basis of Baptist union. In the introduction to his book, he listed five specific convictions he stated that Baptists in the South held at that time, as follows: "(1) the sovereignty of God in salvation; (2) 'the supreme authority of the scripture'; (3) 'the right of each individual to judge for himself in his views of truth as taught in the scriptures'; (4) democratic church government; and (5) believers' baptism."[8]

Later in the same century, the Baptist Union of Great Britain and Ireland affirmed their faith in "the Divine Inspiration and Authority of the Holy Scriptures as the supreme and sufficient rule of our faith and practice: and the right and duty of individual judgment in the interpretation of it."[9]

From our beginnings, Baptists have maintained that each believer has the right and responsibility of personal biblical interpretation. Growing out of our refusal to affirm creeds, we believe that God's Spirit is our sufficient guide in understanding the truth God inspired.

So we encourage every believer to study Scripture personally. Contrary to the institutionalism of the Roman Catholic Church, we have stood for the priesthood of every believer (see chapter two). We do not believe that the church determines the meaning of the Bible, or that church teachings and traditions are on a par with biblical authority. We do not submit to the dictates of denominational officials or decisions. Whenever a Baptist body takes a position on a particular theological subject, it speaks only for those present when the vote was taken. Its resolutions and decisions have no binding authority over any other person or church.

We do not require our members to obtain seminary degrees or acquire ministerial credentials before they interpret Scripture. We do not insist that they agree with their pastor or church leaders theologically. Our churches do not make binding decisions regarding matters of spiritual or theological conviction. There is no particular view of Genesis or Revelation you must affirm to teach the Bible at my church.

Authority relates to salvation and faith

Hugh Wamble was a highly respected church historian at Midwestern Baptist Theological Seminary. In the July 1963 issue of *Foundations* he published one of the most heavily researched articles I have discovered on the subject of Baptists and biblical authority (reprinted in the book, *Proclaiming the Baptist Vision: The Bible*).[10] One hundred and twenty-eight endnotes document every reference from a myriad of Baptist confessions of faith, beginning with the earliest (1610) and extending to the 1963 BF&M. I will not reproduce his citations but will allow his research to guide our own.

Dr. Wamble's article summarizes Baptist confessions regarding three subjects of interest to us here. First, he makes clear that Baptists view biblical authority within the context of salvation and faith. We do not approach Scripture as intending to speak with authority on every subject of human inquiry. We do not see the Bible as God's final word on matters of science, geography, or history. Rather, we view God's word as a means to the end of our personal relationship with him. As we see in the 1963 BF&M, Scripture has "salvation for its end."[11]

Wamble affirms that, "With few exceptions, all of them coming from modern confessions issued by Fundamentalists and Landmarkers, Baptist confessions specify that religion is the area of the Scripture's authority. They do not claim for it authority and infallibility in other areas, nor do they claim that man is able to understand Scripture fully."[12]

This authority is authenticated by "'the inward work of the Holy Spirit,'" as the Holy Spirit bears witness by and with the word in our hearts. This authority does not depend on human testimony, but wholly on God. Neither can this authority be proven by numerous arguments regarding its internal qualities.[13]

Wamble states that biblical authority relates to salvation, as the following phrases from various Baptist confessions indicate:

> *all things "necessary for us to know, and to believe to salvation"; whatsoever is "needfull for us to know, believe, and acknowledge" concerning Christ; "necessary to be known, believed, and observed for Salvation"; "all things necessary to be known for the salvation of men and women"; "all things necessary for salvation"; "all things necessary for his [God's] own Glory, Man's salvation"; "to make men wise unto salvation"; "a sufficient and infallible rule and guide to Salvation"; "salvation for its end. The Scripture's infallibility relates, therefore, to salvation."*[14]

In addition to its authority regarding salvation, the Bible possesses authority in all matters of faith and practice. Again, Wamble states, our confessions make clear our stance:

> *"its [it is] the Scriptures of the Prophets and Apostles that we square our faith and practice by . . . the rule of . . . faith and practice"; "a rule and direction unto us both for faith and practice"; "the rule whereby Saints both in matters of Faith and conversation [conduct] are to be regulated"; "the only rule, and square of our sanctification and obedience in all good works, and piety"; "serving to furnish the man of God for every good work"; "the rule of Faith and Life"; "the . . . only rule of faith and practice"; "the supreme and sufficient rule of our faith and practice"; "the infallible rule of faith and practice"; "the sole authority for faith and practice."* [15]

Included in "practice" are "such things as moral conduct, 'the worship and service of God, and all other Christian duties,' and walking 'together in particular societies, or Churches.'"[16]

We believe the Bible to be our only authority for salvation, faith, and practice. But we do not seek to make it a compendium on science, history, or geography. We know that any book must be interpreted according to its authorial intent. If I use a cookbook to repair a car, I'll not make much progress. The fault is not with the book but its reader.

Primary authority with the New Testament

Dr. Wamble's extensive research summarizes a second area of interest to us: biblical authority rests first with the New Testament. It is not that Baptists consider the Old Testament inferior in any way. Rather, it is completed and fulfilled in the New. So we will read and interpret the Old Testament in light of New Testament revelation. We will seek principles in the Old Testament that are repeated or amplified in the New, and we will resolve to live by their truth. Our primary authority for salvation and faith is the New Testament.

Dr. Wamble states:

> *Primary authority rests with the New Testament. The earliest Baptist confession (1610) says that the proper Christian doctrine for the government of Christ's spiritual kingdom, "so much as is needful for us to*

> *salvation," is written "in the Scripture of the New Testament, whereto we apply whatsoever we find in the canonical book of the Old Testament, which hath affinity and verity." Evidence for Baptists' acceptance of the superior authority of the New Testament may be found in Scripture references, inserted in text and margin, with which confessions are supported.*[17]

Thus, we are New Testament believers. We judge the unclear in light of the clear, and we judge earlier biblical truth in light of later revelation. We believe in *progressive revelation*, the idea that God has progressively revealed himself to us. As a student learns arithmetic before geometry, and trigonometry before calculus, so God revealed himself first in the law and history, then in the prophets, and finally in Christ and the New Testament.

Biblical authority supreme over all others

Dr. Wamble's research speaks with assurance to a third subject: Baptists view biblical authority as preeminent. Citing Baptist statements of faith, Wamble summarizes: "The authority of Scripture means, therefore, that all religious beliefs and practices, whatever they may be and wherever they may be found, must stand under judgment of Scripture."[18]

Baptists view "doctrines of men" as secondary and subsidiary to the truths of Scripture. No person or theological statement can be as important to us as God's revealed word. Baptists have historically stood firmly on this affirmation of biblical authority, and we hold it at the center of our faith and practice.

Statements by Baptist Theologians

A brief survey of renowned Baptist theologians makes clear the consensus Baptists hold on the subject of biblical authority. Let's begin with E. Y. Mullins, president of Southern Baptist Theological Seminary from 1899 to his death in 1928. He taught systematic theology during his tenure as president; served as president of the Southern Baptist Convention from 1921 to 1924; and chaired the committee that drafted the first *Baptist Faith and Message* in 1925.

His systematic theology notes comprised the most formative textbook of its era: *The Christian Religion In Its Doctrinal Expression*. Dr. Mullins concludes his discussion of biblical authority thus:

> *It is a vital and living authority, and not a mechanical and ecclesiastical one. It is our authoritative source of information as to the historical revelation of God in Christ. It is regulative of Christian experience and Christian doctrine. It is the instrument of the Holy Spirit in his regenerative and sanctifying influences. As regulative and authoritative it saves us from subjectivism on the one hand and from a bare rationalism on the other. . . . It is final for us in all the matters of our Christian faith and practice.*[19]

A younger contemporary of Dr. Mullins became the best-known theologian at Southwestern Baptist Theological Seminary in Ft. Worth, Texas. Dr. W. T. Conner's *Christian Doctrine* was considered normative in its field for many years. Dr. Conner, who retired from Southwestern's faculty in 1948, spoke with a definitive voice on all subjects theological.

Dr. Conner made clear his convictions regarding biblical authority. Scripture, he wrote,

> *is authoritative as the voice of God is authoritative to the soul of man. It finds man, searches him, makes him realize his need of spiritual help. If God speaks to man, he must speak in the tones of authority. . . . The God of the Bible is a God of holiness who speaks to man by way of command.*[20]

One of the best-known Baptist theologians of our generation is Millard J. Erickson. His massive *Christian Theology* is required reading for many seminary theology classes. His statement of biblical authority is clear: "Scripture is our supreme legislative authority. It gives us the content of our belief and of our code of behavior and practice."[21] Erickson sees biblical authority as normative for every area of faith and life.

Stanley Grenz, another prolific Baptist theologian, wrote *Theology for the Community of God*, a widely respected textbook in the field. He viewed Scripture as foundational to all theological reflection:

> *In engaging in the theological task, we may simply assume the authority of the Bible on the basis of the integral relationship of theology to the faith community. Because the Bible is the universally-acknowledged foundational document of the Christian church, its message functions as the central norm for the systematic articulation of the faith of that community.*[22]

Russell Dilday, the long-time president of Southwestern Seminary, published in 1982 an outstanding book on the question of biblical authority. In its introduction he describes in pictorial terms the nature of biblical authority for Baptists:

> *The Bible is a factor so central in this denomination's history that Southern Baptists cannot be understood adequately apart from the Book. It is no surprise then that Southern Baptists have traditionally located the pulpits in their churches in the center of the platform, symbolizing the priority given to the proclamation of God's Word. In fact, in some recent church buildings, architects have creatively designed the pulpit to represent the open Bible as the source of the sermon.*[23]

Indeed, the pulpit of the Park Cities Baptist Church in Dallas, where I am privileged to serve as pastor, is designed as an open Bible. The Scriptures are also pictured on the central column of the pulpit, with a gold cross laid across them. Each Sunday I am reminded to stand "in the word" as I preach the crucified and risen Lord. Our church has made graphically clear its commitment to the centrality of biblical authority. Every Baptist church I know would agree.

Conclusion

If you're a Baptist, you stand with a large multitude of people who say with Paul: "All Scripture is God-breathed" (2 Timothy 3:16). We hearken back to a day when no creeds made by human beings existed, when no ecclesiastical authorities or hierarchies had been developed, when churches had no buildings or "clergy"—when we had no authority but God's word.

In the remainder of this book, we'll examine and address the challenges made today to this view of biblical authority. But let's begin by giving thanks for who we are—people of the Book. We stand on the rock of biblical authority, for all other foundations are sinking sand (Matt. 7:24–27).

A boy was fishing early one morning in a dense, cold fog when his boat capsized. In desperation, he spied a rock protruding from the middle of the lake; he swam to it. He huddled on that rock in the bitter cold and fog for more than an hour. Finally a passing fisherman found him. "Weren't you afraid?" he asked the boy. "Yes, sir, I sure did tremble and shake," he admitted, "but the rock never did." It never does.

CHAPTER Two

The Bible Is a Book for All, Not Just a Few

Defending Biblical Authority from the Church

THE CIVIL WAR WAS BY far the deadliest conflict in American history, with some 620,000 killed. I had always assumed the main reason for the horrific casualty count was simply that all who fought were Americans. But then I moved to Atlanta, Georgia, and visited the Atlanta History Center, the most extensive museum in the area devoted to the War Between the States. There I was shocked to discover that twice as many troops died off the battlefield than on it—victims of disease, improperly treated wounds, and exposure.

A quick tour through the medical displays showed why. Rusted handsaws used for amputations; handmade pliers for dentistry; no understanding of germs and little access to anesthesia. Doctors were killed, and untrained soldiers had to take their place.

Today none of us would even think to try the medical procedures these unskilled men and women were forced to attempt. We would never find a book on limb amputation, read what we could, and then do our best. We assume rightly that medicine is best practiced by those who are trained in its specialties. It takes medical school to do medicine.

That's exactly the attitude many take to the Bible today—it takes seminary education and ministerial credentials to understand and apply its truth. The Baptist idea that every believer is a priest unto God, with the right and responsibility of interpreting and living out biblical truth for oneself, is foreign to many who do not share our denominational commitments—and even to many who say they do.

In more than twenty years of pastoral ministry, I have been consistently shocked by the limited time many of my members spend in personal Bible study. In responding to anonymous surveys we have conducted, the number one reason they give is simple: they think they are unqualified. They believe they are unprepared and unskilled to study the Bible for themselves. They consider biblical exposition to be my job. That's why they call professionals and listen to them teach and preach.

We may believe that the Bible is God's authoritative word, but if we don't convince people that they can understand its truths for themselves, our conviction does very little practical good. The pervasive idea that church members cannot really understand Scripture, that they are subject to their religious authorities, is to my mind the most practical problem facing the Baptist doctrine of biblical authority today. Remember, in light of the priesthood of every Christian, you are privileged and responsible to interpret God's word for yourself.

The Illness

The first Christians sparked the greatest spiritual explosion the world has ever seen. By Acts 17:6 they had "turned the world upside down" (KJV). Within a generation, Christians took the gospel to Rome and across the entire Empire. No multiplying movement like it has ever been witnessed.

With growth, however, there are always growing pains. Such pains are made worse when they are misdiagnosed and mistreated.

Here was the problem. As the Christian faith spread beyond its Jewish and Palestinian roots, it began to include people from the far-flung cultures and pagan traditions common to the era. For instance, many of these new converts had been worshipers of Zeus and his corrupt fellow deities. They had learned all kinds of idolatrous rituals and scandalous "worship" practices. Men consorted with the "gods" represented by temple prostitutes. Homosexual as well as heterosexual orgies and drunken feasts were typical ways to honor their chosen deities. Food offered to the gods was then eaten in homes. These converts had no other context for understanding their new faith, and they struggled to break with their pagan culture.

Others were part of the "mystery cults." While we know very little of the practices of these cults (hence their name), we do know that they favored rites and rituals bordering on the occult. One example was the "baptism in blood" by which many of their members were initiated, as they paraded beneath a bull that had been slit so that its entrails and blood poured down on them. This was their concept of "baptism" before coming to Christianity.

Still others were followers of the various schools of Greek philosophy. Plato's Academy argued that the world of "ideas" should be the subject of our attention, not this "shadow" world we can see. The spiritual is good, and the material is bad. The Peripatetic school founded by Aristotle centered on science, logic, biology, and seeking the "idea" in the material. Epicureans taught that proper pleasure is the purpose of life. Stoics believed that fate rules the world (see Acts 17:18). Cynics argued that total withdrawal from life is the only way to happiness. Skeptics claimed that absolute truth is unknowable (a statement they believed absolutely, by the way).

Towering above these various religions, cults, and philosophies was the one religion required across the Empire: the worship of Caesar. The emperor cult had established temples in every major city and most small towns. Civic leaders competed with each other for Roman permission to build the largest temples for the annual required sacrifice to Caesar.

It is no surprise that Paul found Athens to be "full of idols" (Acts 17:16), and could say of her residents, "I see that in every way you are very religious" (Acts 17:22). He could have said the same of every city in the Empire.

Into this maelstrom of confused and competing religions, Jesus sent his people. Their movement became so universal that in three centuries it was the official religion of the Empire and still claims more followers than any other religion on earth.

Now, how was the church to deal with the scandalous, idolatrous ideas and practices its new converts were ready to import into its theology? How were church leaders to protect their movement and members from the crippling malignancy of heresy?

The Diagnosis

An obvious solution soon became clear: restrict the work of theology to those best qualified to interpret the Bible. Empower only the pastors and leaders of the church to teach biblical truth to the rest of the church. Restrict the practice of medicine to those who have completed medical school. Then you'll be able to control and safeguard the theology of the growing Christian movement.

Ignatius (died A.D. 110), bishop of Antioch, was one of the first to argue for the authority of the bishop ("pastor" in Baptist terms) over the church. In his letter to the church at Smyrna, he advised, "Let the laity be subject to the deacons; the deacons to the presbyters; the presbyters to the bishop; the bishop to Christ, even as He is to the Father" (chapter 9). In the same chapter he claimed, "Nor is there any one in the church greater than the bishop, who ministers as a priest to God for the salvation of the whole world." If only the bishop was permitted to interpret Scripture, others could not misunderstand God's word. And so we're safe from heresy.

But what do we do about safeguarding the theology of the bishop? Irenaeus (died A.D. 200 or 203) took Ignatius's concept of pastoral authority a step further, identifying the Roman church as the "preeminent authority" in Christendom. He believed that this church was originally led by Peter and Paul, and that those who succeeded them continued to exercise their spiritual authority. In

Against Heresies (3:3:2), Irenaeus even claimed, "It is a matter of necessity that every Church should agree with this Church, on account of its preeminent authority."

So, if the members of your church will get their biblical interpretation from their pastor, and your pastors will follow the biblical interpretation of the "pastor" of the larger church, you will be protected from idolatry and ignorance. The system is clear and cogent.

Soon Cyprian of Carthage (died about A.D. 258) in North Africa helped make this approach universal. He separated the "clergy" (the *called-out ones*) from the "laity" (from the Greek *laos*, meaning *people*). The job of the clergy is to interpret and apply the Scriptures; the job of the laity is to do what their leaders say. The church, as led by her leaders, is God's means of disseminating his truth. Cyprian's famous claim set the stage for church authority to come: "He can no longer have God for his Father, who has not the Church for his Mother."[1]

The final step came when the Roman emperor Constantine "converted" to Christianity in A.D. 312 (historians still debate the genuineness of his faith). He soon legalized the Christian movement and centered its authority in the church of his capital city. Now the system of institutionalized spiritual control was Empire-wide, with the backing of the Emperor himself.

The church thus had come to view biblical authority as mediated through church teachings. The logic ran like this: God gave us the Bible through the church, and so God will guide the church and her leaders to the proper interpretation and application of his revelation. Creeds, the decisions of church councils, and papal rulings would be the means by which Scripture was to be understood.

Defending the Diagnosis

Of course, Baptists and most other Protestants reject this "two-authority" model. We believe that our sole authority for faith and practice is the Scriptures themselves. But before we critique the church authority model, let's try to understand its appeal today.

First, many of the church's scholars were—and still are—people of excellent academic ability, with deep commitment to biblical truth. Consider Augustine of Hippo (A.D. 354–430), the leading intellectual of his day and one of the greatest Christian thinkers of all time. He took great pains to interpret the Bible as accurately and precisely as possible, producing some of the most in-depth commentaries the church possesses. Baptists would do well to heed his rules for biblical interpretation:

- Trust in Christ personally before you try to understand his word
- Look first for the literal and historical meaning of the passage
- Interpret according to the author's intended meaning
- Study the text within its context
- Use clear passages to interpret the more difficult.

Likewise, Thomas Aquinas (1224?–1274), the leading figure of the medieval church, worked hard to elevate the literal and historical meaning and authority of the biblical text. He argued, "Our faith rests upon the revelation made to the apostles and prophets, who wrote the canonical books, and not on the revelations (if any such there are) made to other doctors."[2] Thomas further asserted that we must not find meanings in Scripture that violate the literal text.[3]

If excellent doctors exist, why do I need to try to learn medicine for myself?

Second, another reason for the appeal of the church authority model is that "lay" people do not know as much about Scripture as trained theologians. I myself spent thirteen years in higher education, earning three theological degrees. I was made to learn Greek, Hebrew, and theological German and Latin. I am now privileged to spend most of my work week studying and teaching God's word. It's hard for members of my church to think they're as qualified to study Scripture as I am.

Third, it's easier to let others interpret the Bible for us. Paul described the Corinthian Christians as "mere infants in Christ," explaining: "I gave you milk, not solid food, for you were not yet ready for it. Indeed, you are still not ready. You are still worldly" (1 Corinthians 3:1–2). Milk is digested food, broken down by the mother so the infant can tolerate it. Many of us want someone else to do the hard work of studying Scripture and give us the essence we need. In our busy lives, we think we're using time more effectively if we pay professionals to interpret the Bible and tell us what we need to know.

Fourth, there is something empowering about being the chief theologian of my faith community. I once heard a leading Baptist pastor call himself the "sole arbiter of theology for my church." I heard another well-known Baptist pastor tell a Sunday School convention that his Bible study leaders teach as an extension of his authority. When you're the only doctor in town, everyone needs you.

So what's wrong with the double authority model? Why not accept a theological world wherein the Scriptures are our authority, but only as they are interpreted and applied by church authority?

The Trouble with the Cure

Any scientist will tell you that a control factor is essential to an effective experiment. There must be baselines of measurement, unchanging standards by which to test theories and formulas. The same is true of theology. When professional theologians are permitted to determine the rules for biblical interpretation, three problems always arise. We cure one disease only to create three others.

Missing the intention of the text

First, trained professionals are not infallible. We can miss the intended meaning of the Scripture, despite our years of study—sometimes, because of them.

For instance, the first problem facing the first Christian theologians was finding ways to use the Old Testament in their new faith. Their typical answer: find Christ in the Hebrew Bible wherever possible. What do we do with those passages and entire books that have little or no intended application to the Messiah? We find him there, anyway.

To locate Jesus on every page of the Old Testament, these interpreters made use of an academic method known as *allegory*. They learned it in school. Jews living in Alexandria, Egypt, centuries before Christ had first begun to adopt this approach to biblical study. They were highly influenced by the worldview of Plato (427–347 B.C.) and his followers, separating the world into the "spiritual" and the "material." They wanted to find the higher, spiritual truths while escaping the "lower" world of material experience.

Applying this approach to the Bible, Jews in Alexandria began to look for ways to find "spiritual" truths in the "material" or "physical" text. Philo (about 20 B.C.–A.D. 50) was their foremost teacher in this regard. Early Christians picked up on the strategy. Let's look at some examples.

Clement of Rome (about A.D. 30–100) said that Rahab's scarlet rope (Joshua 2:21) "made it manifest that redemption should flow through the blood of the Lord to all them that believe and hope in God."[4] Justin Martyr (about A.D. 100–167) insisted that the high priest's bells on his robe (Exodus 28:33–35) symbolized the twelve apostles, each of whom "ring out" the gospel of the Great High Priest.[5] Clement of Alexandria (A.D. 150–213?) thought the different musical instruments in Psalm 150 each symbolized a different part of the human body.[6] In interpreting Jesus' triumphant entry into Jerusalem, Origen (A.D. 185–251?) taught that his colt was the Old Testament carrying him to the cross.[7]

Mistaken interpretation has unfortunately not been reserved for the first centuries of Christian history. When oil wells were first dug in Pennsylvania, many New York ministers opposed the project, claiming that the wells would deplete the oil stored there for the predestined burning of the world (2 Peter 3:10, 12). Church members and leaders rejected the use of winnowing fans in Scotland because "the wind blows where it wills" (John 3:8). Martin Luther reluctantly consented to the bigamous marriage of Philip of Hesse, reasoning that since men such as David and Solomon were permitted more than one wife, such must be biblical.[8]

I often tell my church members that they must judge everything they hear me say by Scripture. The only word God is obligated to bless is his own.

Limiting ministry to ministers

Because the gospel is "the power of God for . . . salvation" (Romans 1:16), it must be studied and shared by the entire church if the entire world is to hear and believe. Limiting Bible study to the professionals is the surest way imaginable to isolate biblical truth from the world. My members will speak with more non-Christians today than I will be privileged to meet this month. If I am the only person permitted to dispense God's word, those who need it most will hear it least.

Imagine a hospital whose chief administrator is the only person allowed to speak with patients. Think of an automobile factory where only the manager is permitted to touch car parts. Suppose that only the head coach got to touch the basketball. You'd have the picture of most churches, with predictable results.

Jesus called his followers the "salt of the earth" and the "light of the world" (Matthew 5:13–16). Salt does no one any good in the saltshaker. Light is no help under the basket. The Bible cannot change the world if it is never taken to it.

Sheep make sheep. Shepherds don't. Jesus wanted disciples to make disciples, Christians to multiply through personal evangelism and ministry. If you were the only believer on the planet today, but you won me to Christ, there would be two disciples. If each of us could win someone to Christ tomorrow, there would be four Christians on the planet. If each of the four could bring someone to Jesus the next day, eight believers would exist. By this process, sixteen Christians would be produced the next day, thirty-two the next, sixty-four the next, and so on. By such multiplication, how long would you guess it would take for the entire world to be won to Christ?

Thirty-four days. As of this writing, the world's population is estimated to be 6,378,974,736. By multiplication, if each Christian won another person to Christ per day, the total in 34 days would be 8,589,934,592. But we can't all win one person a day, you say. Could we win one per year? In thirty-four years the entire planet would know Christ. This kind of multiplying discipleship is how Jesus intended the church to reach the world. His plan still works, but only if we work the plan.

Failing to listen when God speaks to you

Augustine likened the Scriptures to "love letters from home." A good preacher speaks in terms the congregation can understand. A good parent writes letters the children can read.

God intends his people to be able to understand the book he inspired. Not a single verse of a single biblical book requires us to seek the permission of church authorities before we study and apply Scripture for ourselves. There were no such officials for the first generations of the Christian movement.

To the contrary, the Bible is clear regarding its intended interpreter: "All Scripture is God-breathed and is useful for teaching, rebuking, correcting and training in righteousness" (2 Timothy 3:16). For what purpose? "So that the man of God may be thoroughly equipped for every good work" (2 Tim. 3:17). The "man of God," the person to be "thoroughly equipped," requires no ecclesiastical orders, credentials, or ordination. "Every good work" speaks to every dimension of life, whether "clergy" or "lay." This Author intends us all to read and profit from his book.

So the Bible is not like a medical book that requires years of specialized training to understand and apply. Rather, it is more like a first aid handbook written so that anyone in pain can find what is needed. When your foot is cut and you need to know how to stop the bleeding, you don't need a lecture on hematology or a hematologist.

Trying Another Diagnosis

What if the answer to theological heresy isn't less Bible study but more? Maybe the way to prevent interpretive errors is to invite more of God's people to read and understand his word.

That was Martin Luther's approach. He often said the Bible did not need to be defended so much as unleashed. We Baptists understand the sentiment. Here's why.

Just as the double authority model evolved for historical reasons, so our convictions regarding biblical authority have their own history. When we learn why we believe our beliefs, we may hold them with greater conviction, courage, and joy.

Nicholas of Lyra (A.D. 1270–1349), who wrote a commentary on the entire Bible, can help us consider why we believe our beliefs. Nicholas depended on Jewish scholars who interpreted the Bible according to its historical, intended meaning. He accepted the use of other "spiritualizing" methods, but only when they were built on the literal. His interpretive system happened to be used at the University of Erfurt, where a young monk named Martin Luther (1483–1546) would eventually study.

William of Occam (about 1285–1349) likewise asserted that the authority for the Christian life is the Bible, not the church authorities. His position greatly influenced young Luther, who studied under professors influenced by Occam's approach.

Luther in turn made the famous claim, "Only the Holy Scripture possesses canonical authority."[9] He rejected the claims of church authorities, including the pope, to determine the meaning of God's word.[10] Luther's Reformation argued that we should accept *sola scriptura* (only the Bible) as our authority for faith and life.

Luther's six principles for Bible study illustrate his history-making approach to biblical authority:

- We must have a personal commitment to Christ.
- The Bible stands above all church authority and judges our creeds and opinions.
- Bible study must emphasize the historical and grammatical meaning of the text, rejecting all allegory and spiritualizing.
- The Bible can be interpreted by every Christian, without need for church authority or dogma (the corollary of Luther's insistence on the "priesthood of every believer").
- The purpose of all Bible study is to find and trust in Jesus.
- The Old Testament law was given to judge sin; New Testament grace was given to atone for it. We must never understate sin or make grace into works.

Each of these principles is vital for Baptist Bible study today. Each stands on Luther's adamant belief that our only authority is God's word.

John Calvin (1509–64) agreed strongly with Luther: "God bestows the actual knowledge of himself upon us only in the Scriptures,"[11] as "Scripture has its authority from God, not from the Church."[12] He was convinced that the Bible possesses objective meaning and is the final and absolute authority for the Christian life.

From the first Reformers to today, men and women have risked their ministries and even their lives to defend the priority of biblical authority. In a day when church leaders were considered able to bar a soul from heaven, such excommunication was a most serious matter. The first Protestants faced such rejection with courage and conviction. Now, some four centuries later, we who affirm biblical authority owe a debt we can never pay.

Conclusion

In the centuries since the Protestant Reformation, the two authority models we've discussed in this chapter have dominated the Christian faith. Responding to the Protestant Reformation, the Roman Catholic church convened the Council of Trent (1545–63). This Council restated that church teachings and creeds are the basis for all correct Bible study. Protestants have continued our adamant commitment to the Bible as our only authority for faith and practice.

At the end of the day, the issue becomes intensely practical. You may say that you believe the Scriptures to be your only authority and that you do not depend on church teachings and leaders to interpret and apply its truths for you. If, though, you open your Bible only when the professionals discuss its teachings, or consult the professionals before you try to understand the Bible's truths for yourself, your practice contradicts your principles.

How much time do you spend each day in the word of God? What does your answer suggest about what you really believe about biblical authority?

CHAPTER Three

The Bible Is a Trustworthy Book

Biblical Authority and "Contradictions" in Scripture

"The Toddler" has lived up to its name. The Massachusetts Institute of Technology recently unveiled its newest robotic creation at a meeting of the American Association for the Advancement of Science, and the invention performed as planned. Standing knee-high to a human, the device walks more naturally than earlier generations of robots. One day its descendants may be able to walk for days rather than minutes, using simpler mechanisms than in previous creations.

The Toddler and robots of similar design may help scientists develop more natural prosthetic devices for humans, as well as a new generation of robotic help. Unlike the toddlers I remember personally, none is likely to need its diaper changed at two in the morning.

Reading the reports, I am struck with two contradictory emotions. One is awe at human ingenuity, our ability to produce machines of such remarkable sophistication. I wouldn't know the first thing about creating a device that could walk on its own, sensing the floor and adjusting automatically with each step.

At the same time, I am reminded of how little we know. Our greatest scientists, working at the most advanced laboratories in the world, have not been able to produce a device that does what a preliterate baby does naturally. We can walk in space, but we cannot imitate completely the walk of an infant. We can create computers with which to write these words, but we cannot create a living blade of grass.

For all our scientific progress, our minds are still finite and fallen. Our test tubes cannot show us what lies beyond death, on the other side of this brief moment we call life. Our proven knowledge is limited to the tiny slice of reality we can experience in this moment. For the eternal questions, we need knowledge beyond our time-conditioned world. We need a relationship with the Creator who transcends his creation. We need to trust the One no test tube can contain, the Person no laboratory logic can fathom.

But we keep trying to prove such eternal matters. We want life to make sense. We believe that non-contradiction is the test for truth, that logic and reason are the way forward. So, when we find apparent contradictions in our laboratories or our Bibles, we protest. *The Bible is filled with contradictions*, we often hear. Such criticism justifies the skepticism about biblical authority that is so common today. Why do we think in this way? What are we to believe about the Bible and "contradictions"? Why does the subject matter?

The Contradictory History of Contradictions

Everyone knows that contradictions are bad. If you can find a statement I make in this chapter that disagrees with something I've already said, you'll feel justified in rejecting both. Even though one may be right. Even though they both may be. Why?

We have Aristotle (384–322 B.C.) to thank, or blame. In his desire to compile all knowledge into an organized system, he devised laws of logic as organizational tools. One of them is called the *law of contradiction*. It goes as follows: *A* cannot equal *B* and at the same time not equal *B*.

From then to now, we Westerners have adopted Aristotle's law as the basis for determining all truth. If we can find a contradiction in the Bible, we think we have reason to dismiss the Bible's veracity. But before we decide we're right, let's think about Aristotle's laws some more.

Aristotle's approach is necessary in the physical sciences. We want our doctors to diagnose ailments by Aristotelian logic. If your knee is hurting, you don't want your orthopedist to suggest that it might be both cancer and torn cartilage, and so let's treat it for both and see what happens. You want a non-contradictory medical response.

The trouble with Aristotle's law comes when we apply it outside its intended context. Aristotle wanted to classify all empirical knowledge, and he needed his laws of logic to do so. But he didn't use these laws outside the physical realm. When we apply them outside the physical realm, problems quickly emerge.

Relational experience is seldom logical and non-contradictory. It may appear contradictory to claim that you love your children and yet sometimes wish they'd never been born. But if you're a typical parent, both are sometimes true. Jesus claimed to be fully God and fully human; God is three and yet one; the Bible is divinely inspired but humanly written; God knows the future, but we have freedom to choose. Inside every essential Christian doctrine is a paradox, an apparent contradiction.

This is as it should be. If you and I could understand fully the nature of God, either God wouldn't be God or we would be. We should expect paradox and rational tensions within our finite, fallen understanding of the omnipotent God of the universe.

Many of the so-called contradictions in the Bible fit into such spiritual or relational categories. For instance, the Bible teaches that "God is love" (1 John 4:8). Yet the Bible also states clearly, "The wrath of God is being revealed from heaven against all the godlessness and wickedness of men who suppress the truth by their wickedness" (Romans 1:18). Too, the Bible warns, "For those who are self-seeking and who reject the truth and follow evil, there will be wrath and anger" (Romans 2:8). How can God both love and hate? Don't ask Aristotle. But you can ask any parent.

Not all truth fits into test tubes. My seventh-grade geometry teacher claimed that parallel lives never intersect. But to prove it, he'd have to draw them forever. Black and white are not the only crayons in the box.

Consider the Larger Context

A second category of apparent contradictions in the Bible results from misunderstanding the intended context of the texts in question. Let's look at some commonly-cited examples, taking them in the order they appear in Scripture.

An eye for an eye and the God of love

A critic says, *The Old Testament teaches, "An eye for an eye and a tooth for a tooth." But Jesus told us to turn the other cheek. Which is right?* Both.

We're dealing with the *lex talionis*, the oldest law in the world. It appears in the Code of Hammurabi, dated in the eighteenth century B.C. This law is found in the Old Testament as well: "If there is serious injury, you are to take life for life, eye for eye, tooth for tooth, hand for hand, foot for foot, burn for burn, wound for wound, bruise for bruise" (Exodus 21:23-25).

Before this law, if I wrecked your car you could destroy my house. If I injured your child, you could kill all my children. The original purpose of the law was thus to limit vengeance. Only the one who caused the injury could be punished, not his entire family or tribe. Too, he could be punished only to the degree that he had injured another, thus protecting him from a more powerful enemy. This law did not promote retribution; rather, it limited it.

But the law seems to contradict Jesus' clear teaching in the Sermon on the Mount: "Do not resist an evil person. If someone strikes you on the right cheek, turn to him the other also. And if someone wants to sue you and take your tunic, let him have your cloak as well. If someone forces you to go one mile, go with him two miles. Give to the one who asks you, and do not turn away from the one who wants to borrow from you" (Matt. 5:39–42).

In their historical context, Jesus' statements are intended to speak to a very different subject than self-defense and retribution. Each of Jesus' examples points to the same principle: stop the cycle of revenge. Don't return slander with slander, gossip with gossip.

His first example relates to your *honor*: "If someone strikes you on the right cheek, turn to him the other also" (Matt. 5:39). "Strikes" in the original means *to slap*. The right hand was the only one used in public. To slap your right cheek with my right hand, thus back-handed, was an insult, not a threat to life and limb. Jesus says, *Don't slap back. If someone insults you, don't insult them.*

Next, Jesus speaks of your *possessions*: "If someone wants to sue you and take your tunic, let him have your cloak as well" (Matt. 5:40). Your "tunic" was your undershirt with sleeves; it could be taken in a lawsuit. Your "cloak" could not, for it protected you from the elements. But give it anyway. Don't insist on your rights.

Now Jesus deals with your *time*: "If someone forces you to go one mile, go with him two miles" (Matt. 5:41). Jesus refers to the power of a Roman soldier to make a Jew carry his military pack for one mile. Carry it two miles. Sacrifice the time, although you don't have to. Do it anyway.

Last, Jesus speaks to your money: "Give to the one who asks you, and do not turn away from the one who wants to borrow from you" (Matt. 5:42). As Augustine reminds us, we are not told to give everything we are asked for, but to give to every person who asks. Even though it is your right not to.

So refuse retribution. Stop the cycle of vengeance. Don't repeat the gossip or slander. Refuse to return insult for insult, pain for pain. It has been noted that an eye for an eye and a tooth for a tooth is a rapid way to a sightless, toothless world. That's the point of Jesus' teaching, and it in no way contradicts the law in Exodus. The former deals with personal insults, and the latter with physical malice. Knowing the context explains the "contradiction."

Abiathar and Ahimelech

In Mark 2, Jesus defended his disciples' decision to eat grain on the Sabbath: "Have you never read what David did when he and his companions were hungry and in need? In the days of Abiathar the high priest, he entered the house of God and ate the consecrated bread, which is lawful only for priests to eat. And he also gave some to his companions" (Mark 2:25–26). But 1 Samuel 21:1 says that this occurred when Ahimelech, Abiathar's father, was priest. For such kindness to David, Ahimelech and his family were killed by Saul's soldiers. His son Abiathar escaped and was later made priest (1 Sam. 22:20–23).

This problem is explainable on grammatical terms. "In the days of Abiathar" translates a Greek phrase that says literally "*upon* Abiathar the high priest." Mark usually uses "upon" (*epi* in Greek) to refer to location rather than time. The phrase is better translated, "at the place where Abiathar was high priest," not "during the time when" he served.[1]

Another so-called contradiction involving these two men is also explainable. Second Samuel 8:16–18 lists King David's officials and includes "Ahimelech son of Abiathar" as priest (8:17). We know from 1 Samuel 22:20 that Ahimelech was Abiathar's father. But it is possible that Abiathar had a son whom he named for his own father Ahimelech. Remember that Zechariah's family wanted to name his son for his father, until his parents insisted that he be called "John" (Luke 1:59–63). My middle name is my grandfather's first name; one of my sons carries his grandfather's first name as well. Such family traditions are still as common today as in the ancient world.

Quirinius, Governor of Syria

Luke 2:2 tells us that the census that led Joseph and Mary to Bethlehem "was the first census that took place while Quirinius was governor of Syria." However, Jewish and Roman historical records seem to date Quirinius's term in office A.D. 6–9. Can we reconcile the discrepancy?

Yes. We know from the Roman historian Tacitus (*Annals*, Book III) that Quirinius led military expeditions in Cilicia, which adjoins Syria, a decade earlier. Luke uses "governor" (Greek, *hegemoneuo*) in a general sense of leading or ruling. So Luke may well have this military office in mind. Too, some ancient records seem to indicate that Quirinius served two terms in office; the first from 6–4 B.C. and the second from A.D. 6–9. A census occurred during each term (Acts 5:37 refers to the census that took place during Quirinius's second term in office).

It seems unlikely that Luke would make an historical error regarding political leadership at the time of Jesus' birth, given his careful use of eyewitness records (Luke 1:1–4) and the fact that such a mistake would be exposed easily by his contemporaries. But given the general nature of Luke's word "governor," it is easy to see how his narrative correlates with ancient historical records.

In a sermon this Sunday, I could attribute the allied victory in World War II to the "leadership" of Dwight Eisenhower, even though Franklin Roosevelt and Harry Truman were President during this time and Eisenhower came to the White House later. If I state that General Eisenhower was President in 1945, any who listen to my sermon would quickly correct me. If I call him our "leader," all would understand.

Mark 1, Isaiah, and Malachi

Mark 1:2–3 begins the life of Jesus with this citation:

> *It is written in Isaiah the prophet: "I will send my messenger ahead of you, who will prepare your way"—"a voice of one calling in the desert, 'Prepare the way for the Lord, make straight paths for him.'"*

The problem is that the first citation does not come from Isaiah but from Malachi 3:1. Did Mark make a mistake? No.

Mark's second citation is taken directly from Isaiah 40:3, so that the prophecy he cites did in fact come from Isaiah. But what of the first prediction? Isaiah was the first book in the division of the

Hebrew Bible known as the Latter Prophets, so that everything from Isaiah to Malachi could be considered to be "in Isaiah.'

This kind of attribution was common in ancient literature. For instance, the Book of Proverbs begins, "The proverbs of Solomon son of David, king of Israel." Yet Proverbs 30 claims to be "the sayings of Agur son of Jakeh" (Prov. 30:1), while Proverbs 31 is the work of "King Lemuel" (Prov. 31:1). The larger book is attributed to Solomon, since he is its principal and best-known author. In the same way, the prophecies found in the Latter Prophets all stand "in" or under Isaiah, their first and best-known representative.

The roof and the paralytic

Mark informs us that the friends of a paralyzed man tried to bring him to Jesus, but they could not get inside the house crowded with people listening to him teach. So "they made an opening in the roof above Jesus and, after digging through it, lowered the mat the paralyzed man was lying on" (Mark 2:4). Mark describes a typical Palestinian house, made with a flat roof accessible by a ladder. Usually roofing clay was packed and rolled. Then it was covered with branches laid across wooden beams.

However, Luke describes the same event this way: "they went up on the roof and lowered him on his mat through the tiles into the middle of the crowd" (Luke 5:19). Since Gentile houses often used such tiles, could it be that Luke used a description with which he was more familiar? If so, was he in error? Did the friends "dig through" a clay roof, or remove ceiling tiles?

Perhaps both. Jesus was teaching in a house large enough to accommodate a crowd that included Pharisees and teachers of the law "from every village of Galilee and from Judea and Jerusalem" (Luke 5:17). Perhaps this expansive house was owned by a person wealthy enough to afford roof tiles, rather than the cheaper thatched roof that had to be replaced periodically. These tiles would substitute for the branches that were laid on wooden beams across the clay roof. Mark does not state that the friends dug through branches but only through the roof itself. Luke gives us the added detail that they removed tiles before they dug through the clay roof. There is no reason to conclude that the two accounts contradict each other.

Angels at Easter

At Jesus' resurrection, when the women came to the empty tomb "two men in clothes that gleamed like lightning stood beside them" (Luke 24:4). John's account agrees: Mary "saw two angels in white, seated where Jesus' body had been, one at the head and the other at the foot" (John 20:12). However, Matthew 28:2–7 records only one angel who rolled back the stone, frightened the guards, and spoke to the women. Too, Mark tells us that the women found "a young man dressed in a white robe sitting on the right side" of the tomb (Mark 16:5).

Were there two angels or one at the resurrection? Yes. In ancient literature, it was common for the spokesman to be described without mentioning those who accompanied him. For instance, in Acts 15 we learn that Silas accompanied Paul on his second missionary journey (Acts 15:40). But then Luke records, "He went through Syria and Cilicia, strengthening the churches" (Acts 15:41), and then "He came to Derbe and then to Lystra" (Acts 16:1). Where was Silas? Silas was with Paul, although unnamed and unmentioned.

In the same way, one angel could roll aside the stone and speak to the women, while another was present as well. The accounts do not necessarily contradict each other. Additionally, the angels were seated (John 20:12) and standing (Luke 24:4), as they changed their posture during the course of the event.

Such independence of accounts actually strengthens the case for biblical trustworthiness. It is obvious that the writers did not try to coordinate their descriptions. No collusion was at work. Any traffic officer will testify that two people who witness the same automobile accident will tell the story with different details. As long as they agree on the essentials, their testimony will be accepted as trustworthy. In fact, if every detail agrees, the court will wonder whether the witnesses coordinated their stories before telling them under oath.

In the same way, we can know that those who recorded the first Easter got the intended meaning and message of the resurrection right. To ask more is to raise a question the text is not intended to answer.

Understand the Author's Intention

A third category of supposed contradictions results from misunderstanding the background behind passages in God's word. When we don't have the full picture, we distort the parts we do see.

It is unfair to any book to ask questions it does not intend to answer. We don't use a cookbook to repair a car, or a poem to mow the lawn. If a biblical writer did not intend chronological, historical, geographic, or scientific precision, it is unfair to criticize him for failing by such standards. A meteorologist can predict the time of tomorrow's "sunrise" without intending to take us back to the Ptolemaic universe in which the sun rotates around the earth.

Let's consider some examples of seeming contradictions that are explained by remembering the intention of the biblical authors.

Jesus' temptations

Matthew 4 records Jesus' temptations in this order: turn stones into bread (Matt. 4:3); jump from the temple (Matt. 4:5–6); and worship Satan on a mountain (Matt. 4:9). Luke 4 records the same temptations, but in a different order: turn stones to bread (Luke 4:3); worship the devil on a mountain (Luke 4:5–6); and jump from the temple (Luke 4:9–11).

Aristotelian logic requires that we ask, *Which order is correct? Which writer is wrong?* If one is wrong, maybe they're both wrong. Maybe Satan is mythical. Maybe Jesus' temptations are symbolic. Once we start down the slippery slope of contradiction, where do we stop?

In their intentional context, there is no such contradiction here. Neither Matthew nor Luke claimed to be writing historical chronology, and so the order of Jesus' temptations is immaterial to their purpose.

Let's say a staff member asks me what I did today, and I tell him that I taught Men's Bible Study this morning, attended our Thursday prayer meeting, and worked on my sermon for this weekend. Then tonight my wife asks me what I did, and I tell her that I taught Men's Bible Study, worked on my sermon, and attended Thursday prayer meeting. Have I contradicted myself? Only if I promised to state the activities in their proper chronological order each time I recounted the events. If such was not my intention, my retelling of the day is correct in each account.

In the same way, Matthew and Luke contradict each other regarding Jesus' temptations only if each of them stated their intention to record chronological precision. Since they don't, it is clear that the order of the temptations stands outside their intention and thus our criticism.

Copyist errors

The Bible is the product of some fifteen centuries of authorship and another fifteen centuries of handwritten transmission. Not until the Gutenberg Bible was it possible to copy and transmit the Scriptures mechanically; not until our own generation was such possible electronically.

As we will see in chapter four, the manuscripts for the biblical texts are astoundingly accurate and trustworthy. However, it is inevitable that human hands, copying such a large text, would make occasional scribal errors.

Let's look at some apparent contradictions that result from copyist errors. Second Samuel 10 tells us that in conflict with the Aramean army, "David killed seven hundred of their charioteers" (2 Sam. 10:18). When 1 Chronicles 19 records the same event four centuries later, it states, "David killed seven thousand of their charioteers" (19:18). It would be easy for a scribe to make a mistake by either reducing the 1 Chronicles number or adding to the one recorded in 2 Samuel.

Of course, the two accounts are not technically in contradiction, since 700 is a subset of 7,000. David killed 700 charioteers if he killed 7,000. But most likely the difference is the result of a copyist mistake. This mistake changes absolutely nothing about the intended message of the two passages—David led his armies to victory and his nation to peace.

Another example of copyist error is in the well-known Twenty-third Psalm. The NIV renders the last phrase, "and I will dwell in the house of the Lord forever" (Ps. 23:6). The Masoretes (scribes who copied the Old Testament) rendered the verb as "I will return," from the Hebrew verb *wesabti*. But the verb *weyasabti* ("remain") was likely the original. The *w* (Hebrew *waw*) and the *y* (Hebrew *yod*) looked so much alike that the Masoretes probably saw the *y* as a repeated *w* and dropped it, rendering the verb *wesabti*. Because Hebrew scholars believe the original verb was *weyasabti*, they translate the phrase "I will dwell."

Before you decide that these kinds of mistakes in transmission disqualify biblical authority, apply such a test to any other means of communication. A single typographical error in tomorrow's newspaper would mean that you cannot trust anything it reports. One mistake in tonight's television newscast would mean that every story is unreliable. One mistake in spelling or syntax would disqualify everything you read in this book.

By such standards no literature or communication medium can be trusted. No phone book or dictionary should be consulted. No doctor should practice medicine, since medical books are not free from error. Too, no medical practice is immune from mistakes. If a single doctor misdiagnoses a single ailment, none of us should ever consult a physician again.

At issue is the intention of the text. As we will see in chapter nine, the Bible does not intend to be a book that meets twenty-first century standards of scientific, geographic, or historical precision. No ancient book does. Furthermore, few if any documents in current literature can stand such scrutiny perfectly. But the Bible, as transmitted to us across thirty-five centuries, retains complete accuracy in all it intends to accomplish. It shows us how to find Jesus

(John 20:30–31) and how to be equipped for faith and service in the kingdom of God (2 Timothy 3:16–17).

Conclusion

The next time you hear someone claim the Bible is full of contradictions, ask whether he or she has read the Bible. Then ask whether it is a contradiction for a person to dismiss a book he or she hasn't read. Now offer to help the person study the Bible and meet its Author. It is a contradiction to me that a holy and perfect God would want me to live in God's perfect paradise. I'm glad it's not to him.

CHAPTER Four

The Bible Is Confirmed by Internal Evidence

Biblical Authority and Manuscript Evidence

IT'S BEEN SAID THAT A guess repeated three times is a fact. The more we repeat what we hear, the more we tend to embellish the report with our own opinions. That's just human nature.

Perhaps you've played the "repeating game." Get thirty or so people to sit in a circle. Whisper a few sentences of a newsworthy nature to the person on your right, and ask that person to repeat what you just said to the next person. Then that person is to repeat the news to the next, and so on. When the report comes back to you, it will bear little resemblance to the news that started the game.

I was a first-year seminary student working part-time as a graphic artist. One day a colleague asked me a question I'd not considered in the eight years I'd been a Christian: "Why do you believe the Bible? You know it was copied by hand for centuries, don't you? What you have can't possibly be accurate. How can you trust it?" I didn't know what to say. Would you?

One of the many damaging claims of Dan Brown's bestselling novel, *The Da Vinci Code,* is this assertion, made by a fictional "historian" but carrying the claim of truth:

> *The Bible is a product of* man, *my dear. Not of God. The Bible did not fall magically from the clouds. Man created it as a historical record of tumultuous times, and it has evolved through countless translations, additions, and revisions. History has never had a definitive version of the book.*[1]

Note that Mr. Brown claims for his work, "All descriptions of artwork, architecture, documents, and secret rituals in this novel are accurate."[2] Tragically, multiplied thousands who read his novel assume that his assertion regarding the documents of the Bible is true. I have spoken with many Christians who don't agree with Mr. Brown but don't know why.

The bad news is that not many believers know where the Bible came from. We don't know how to defend its trustworthiness against the accusations made by my colleague years ago. But here's the good news. When we learn how the Bible was created and transmitted to us, we discover yet another reason to trust its authority in our lives today.

How the Bible Was Created

Paul was locked away in a cold, damp Roman prison. When he wrote to Timothy, his young apprentice, he could have asked for anything. Better food, more companions, lawyers to plead his case, the church to rally to his defense. Instead, here is his personal appeal: "When you come, bring the cloak that I left with Carpus at Troas, and my scrolls, especially the parchments" (2 Timothy 4:13). What were his "scrolls" and "parchments"? Why did they matter so much to history's greatest apostle?

The materials of the Bible

Scrolls were made of papyrus, the most prevalent "paper" in the ancient world. The papyrus reed grew along the Nile River in Egypt and in other marshy places. It was cut, unrolled, and left to dry in the sun. Strips were laid horizontally, and then others were overlaid vertically. They were woven and glued together, constituting the most common and inexpensive writing material of the day. These sheets were then sewn or glued together into scrolls.

A more expensive and durable writing material was parchment, named for the region of Pergamum in Asia Minor (modern-day western Turkey), where it was developed. This was manufactured from animal skins, usually sheep or goats (vellum). Like papyrus, it was often rolled into scrolls.

Reeds were used as brushes, with a kind of carbon-liquid glue as ink. Such pen and ink was employed with papyrus and parchment.

The original books of the Bible were apparently all written on papyrus. Since this first "paper" decayed quickly, none of these original writings exist today. The same is true for the writings of Plato, Aristotle, or Julius Caesar. We simply don't have the originals of ancient books but must rely on copies made through the centuries.

Around A.D. 100, people began cutting scrolls into sheets and stitching them together. The result was the "codex," the ancestor to our book. Codexes using parchment are the earliest copies of the complete New Testament that we have today.

The scrolls and parchments Paul requested were his Bible and his books. They were the earliest form of the Scriptures we cherish and study today. If you were locked away on death row, would they be your first request?

The languages of the Bible

God's word has come to us in three original languages. Hebrew is the oldest of the three, the language used for most of the Old Testament. It is written from right to left, with no upper or lower case letters or vowels. Centuries later, scribes added the vowels (called "points") we have in the Hebrew Bible today.

Aramaic was a descendant of Hebrew. It was the common spoken language of the Jews toward the end of the Old Testament era, and it was the typical language of Jesus' culture. It is found in the Old Testament in Ezra 4:8–6:18, where the author draws on documents exchanged by the Persian king and his subjects; Ezra 7:12–26, recording a letter from the Persian king to Ezra; and Daniel 2:4—7:28.

Jesus and his disciples could read Hebrew. For instance, Jesus read from the Isaiah scroll, written in Hebrew, before preaching at Nazareth (Luke 4:17–19). However, Jesus and the disciples typically would have spoken in Aramaic. We still find Aramaic words in the Gospels—"Abba" for Father (Mark 14:36), and "Eloi, Eloi, lama sabachthani!" (Mark 15:34, "My God, my God, why have you forsaken me!"), for instance.

Greek was the universal written language of the Roman Empire, and thus the language in which the entire New Testament was written. There were two kinds of Greek in the first century—the classical language employed by the cultured, and the *koine* ("common") Greek used by the masses.

A century ago, scholars were confused by the contrast between the Greek of the New Testament and that found in the classical writers. But then archaeologists began discovering scraps of papyrus and pieces of pottery from the first century, written in the more common language of the people. Shopping lists, personal letters, wills, and documents came to light. Their language was strikingly similar to that of the New Testament.

Today scholars rank the language of the New Testament documents on a spectrum relative to *koine* and classical Greek literature. The Gospels are the most "common" in nature, containing so much of Jesus' discourse with the masses and intended for the widest distribution. First Peter (written by Silvanus from dictation by Peter, 1 Peter 5:12) and Hebrews use the most classical Greek language in the New Testament. Luke and Acts are somewhere in the middle.

William Barclay concludes, "It is worthwhile remembering that the New Testament is written in colloquial Greek; it is written in the kind of Greek a man in the street wrote and spoke in the first century. . . . Anything that makes the New Testament sound other than contemporary mistranslates it."[3]

It is a miracle that God could take on human flesh, that the Creator would enter his Creation. It is also a miracle that God would give us his revelation in our language, and that the Lord of the universe would write a book we could read. But this is precisely what the Lord has done. The wisdom of the ages has been transmitted on papyrus and parchment, in human languages through human instruments. We could not climb up to God, and so God climbed down to us.

Getting as Close as Possible

Now, how can we be sure that we have what God, the Author, wrote? As we have noted, no original documents for any ancient book exist today. Imagine storing newspapers in the elements for a year, much less a century or millennium. In addition, there was no way to distribute the biblical writings apart from copying them by hand. In the era before movable printing, scribes were the first publishers. How do we know that they copied the Bible accurately?

The work of textual critics

"Textual critics" are scholars who devote themselves to studying copies of ancient literature, seeking to develop a version that is as close to the original as possible. Textual critics work with the manuscripts of Shakespeare, for instance, debating which passages came from the playwright himself, which to attribute to Christopher Marlowe, and so on. Scholars study the copies of works by Plato and Aristotle, seeking to determine which are closest to the originals.

Textual critics do the same hard, crucial work with the Scriptures. Their work is scientific and precise. We can trust their conclusions as the product of objective scholarship.

Textual criticism works best when two circumstances prevail: (1) numerous ancient copies; (2) as close in time to the original writings as possible. The fewer the ancient copies, the less material the scholars have to use. The larger the time gap between the original and our earliest copies, the greater margin for undiscoverable error in transmission.

The Bible and other ancient literature

What copies of famous ancient literature do we possess today? Caesar's *Gallic Wars* was composed between 58 and 50 B.C. Our oldest copies of it were made 900 years later; we have only nine or ten good manuscripts. We have no independent verification for much of Caesar's descriptions except the book itself. Tacitus was the most famous historian of ancient Rome. His descriptions of first-century life in the Empire are considered the most authoritative histories we have. However, of the fourteen books of his *Histories*, only four and one-half survive today. Our earliest copies were made 900 years after the originals. The *History of Thucydides* was written around 400 B.C. Our earliest complete manuscript dates to 1,300 years later. We have only five or so copies of any work of Aristotle (384–322 B.C.), the earliest of which was made 1,400 years after the originals.

By contrast, our oldest complete New Testament was made just 300 years after the original. One papyrus (known as P^{52}) contains a section from John 18, and dates to A.D. 130 (just thirty-five or so years after John's original).[4]

No other ancient book comes close to the Bible with regard to the number and quality of manuscript copies in existence today. The sheer weight of evidence is strongly in favor of biblical trustworthiness and authority.

Studying the copies we have

Historians possess more than 5,000 Greek manuscripts of the New Testament, and more than 10,000 copies in other ancient languages. They classify these copies by age and writing materials, and whether they used upper or lower case letters. They also group manuscripts by the geographic centers where they were produced—Alexandria, Egypt; Caesarea in Palestine; Antioch of Syria; Constantinople; and Rome.

Textual critics consider a number of factors in determining which manuscripts are oldest and closest to the originals. They examine the chronological appearance of the document—its apparent age and the period when it first came into use. They investigate the geographical circulation of the manuscript, the extent of its usage, and the number of times the document was copied, on the assumption that the more widely accepted the document, the more likely it was considered reliable by its audience. They look for agreement between the manuscript and quotations found in the church fathers.

Too, they investigate the historical "genealogy" of the manuscript's textual tradition. Scholars know that documents originating in Alexandria, for instance, possess certain advantages and flaws. Each geographic center manifests its own techniques and characteristics in copying and transmission.

Unintentional errors

Much of the work of textual critics consists in identifying the presence of scribal, editorial, and/or translator errors.[5] Scholars have identified four kinds of unintentional errors as most common, and watch for them with special interest.

Some mistakes arose from faulty eyesight—failing to distinguish between similar letters and other similar matters. For instance, the Hebrew *y* (*yodh*) looks much like the *w* (*waw*). Too, the Greek capital letters for *epsilon* (made as a rounded *E*) and *theta* (an oval with a line in the middle) are very similar when handwritten.

Haplography occurred when a scribe wrote once what should have been written twice (like "maping" for "mapping" in English). *Dittography* occurred when the scribe wrote twice what should have been written only once. Another related mistake resulted from changing the proper order of letters or words.

A second kind of error resulted from faulty hearing, when the scribe made copies from dictation or even pronounced the words to himself as he wrote them. *Homophony* occurred when the scribe wrote a wrong word that sounded the same as the correct term (like *two* for *to* in English).

A third category of scribal mistakes was errors of the mind. The scribe held a phrase in his memory as he copied it, and sometimes transposed or missed letters or words as a result. Mistakes of this type fall into several categories:

- Changing the proper order of letters or words
- Combining the last letter of a word with the first letter of the following word, or combining two words into one
- Separating one word improperly into two
- Missing the words between two phrases that end in the same way (When the scribe looked from the original to the copy he was writing and then looked back to the original, his eyes could easily fall on the latter ending and miss that which came in between.)
- Similarly, missing the intervening words if two phrases began in the same way

A fourth kind of unintentional error resulted from mistakes in scribal judgment. Words and notes made in the margin of the older copy were sometimes incorporated into the text of the new manuscript. Scribes would occasionally copy across two columns of a text, rather than working down the passage a column at a time.

Intentional changes

At times, scribes tried to "clean up" the text before them by making deliberate changes to the manuscript at hand. If a scribe felt the style of his text could be improved, he would sometimes make grammatical "corrections." Parallel texts in the Gospels were often harmonized to agree completely with each other. New Testament quotes of Old Testament texts were "improved" to conform to the Septuagint (the Greek Old Testament).

"Conflation" was a common problem. When a scribe worked from two or more manuscripts and found variant readings, he would sometimes include both in his copy. Too, some scribes added doctrinal statements according to their convictions. For instance, one amended Luke's statement, "It seemed good also to me to write an orderly account" (Luke 1:3) to read, "It seemed good also to me and to the Holy Spirit" (see Acts 15:28, "It seemed good to the Holy Spirit and to us. . . .").

Determining the best manuscripts

We should expect such errors to creep into the handwritten copies of any ancient book. The more copies we have, the more likely it is that we will find such errors. Watching for such common mistakes is the first step to finding them in a particular text. Then scholars are able to deal with these mistakes, developing a text that is as close to the original as possible.

How do textual critics do this work? They follow certain established rules. Here is the procedure for the Old Testament suggested by Ernst Wurthwein and followed widely by scholars:

- When the Masoretic Text (the most reliable Old Testament text) has been preserved without a variant, and there are no other manuscripts that differ, we must accept the reading as proper.
- When the Masoretic Text and other manuscripts support different readings, the MT is to be preferred wherever appropriate.
- When the Masoretic Text and other manuscripts support different but apparently equally possible or plausible readings, determine which reading is more difficult (see below) or most likely explains the other versions.
- Pay close attention to psychological and/or theological reasons why a particular scribe or school might preserve the text in a particular way.
- When no clear conclusion can be made based on manuscript evidence, suggest a conjectural solution which seems closest to the intention of the author of the text.[6]

In describing the work of New Testament textual criticism, Bruce Metzger outlines the procedures typically followed.[7] First, consider external evidence. How old is the document? What type does it embody? Next, examine the text itself. In general, when variances occur we are to prefer the more difficult reading. We assume that the scribe would more likely resolve apparent contradictions within the text.

We are to prefer the shorter reading to the longer, assuming that the scribes would more likely add explanatory phrases than omit portions of the text. We will assume that a version that harmonizes parallel accounts is more likely the product of scribal changes than one that is distinct from the other versions.

In addition, we are to consider:

- The style and vocabulary of the author throughout his work
- The immediate context
- Harmony with the usage of the author elsewhere, and in the Gospels
- The Aramaic background of Jesus' teaching
- The priority of the Gospel of Mark (probably the first to be written)
- The influence of the Christian community on the formulation and transmission of the passage in question

With these rules in place, textual critics go about the painstaking task of comparing the multiplied thousands of ancient copies of Scripture. The result is that we have a Bible that is trustworthy in every matter of faith and practice.

The Dead Sea Scrolls

As a case in point, consider the Dead Sea Scrolls. Prior to their discovery in the caves at Qumran, the oldest complete copy of the Old Testament known to scholars dated to the tenth century. When a shepherd looking for a lost sheep found the first of the scrolls in 1947, the most dramatic discovery in the history of biblical archaeology and manuscripts resulted. We now possess Old Testament manuscripts dating back to the first century before Christ. The Dead Sea Scrolls contain every book of the Old Testament except Esther. They take us a thousand years closer to the originals.

How close was the Masoretic Text to these documents? In other words, how accurate were the scribes who copied the text for a thousand years? The results are amazing. There is word-for-word accuracy in the vast majority of the texts. The variations that remain are the results of obvious scribal errors.

The scribes who transmitted the Bible across the centuries before printing was available did their work with astounding accuracy. Their work, while not perfect, was far closer than the manuscript copyists for any other ancient book. With the help of textual scholars, we today possess an Old Testament that is virtually identical to the originals. And the Greek New Testament we have today is likewise accurate and trustworthy.

Why So Many Versions?

If the biblical text produced by scholars is so close to the original, why do we need so many translations of the Bible? And why do modern versions differ from the King James Version?

The KJV translators used the *textus receptus* (the "received text"), the best version of the Bible available when they did their work in the early 17th century. This Greek text was based on the scholarship of Erasmus, who published his first Greek New Testament in 1516. He based his work on the six manuscripts that happened to be available to him at the time.

Robert Estienne[8] then produced a Greek New Testament in 1550 that relied heavily on the Greek text of Erasmus.[9] The preface to an edition in 1633 by Estienne's son Henri states, "You have therefore the text received by all; in which we give nothing altered or corrupt." From this claim came the term "received text" or *textus receptus.* Thus the *textus receptus* became the standard for translators of the Greek New Testament across the next three centuries.

Then some remarkable discoveries changed the course of Bible translation forever.

- The most dramatic was Codex (meaning *book*) Sinaiticus. This is a parchment copy of the entire Greek Bible (although some of the OT has been lost). The copy dates to the fourth century A.D. It was discovered by Count Tischendorf in the Mount Sinai Monastery in 1844. After two other trips to the monastery, he was able to purchase the codex for the Russian tsar in 1859. The British government bought the book from the Soviet Union for 100,000 pounds in 1933. It resided for many years in the British Museum, and is now on display at the British Library. The same library also houses Codex Alexandrinus. This copy of the Greek Bible was made in the fifth century, and was presented to England's King Charles I in 1627 by the Patriarch of Alexandria.
- The Vatican Library houses Codex Vaticanus. This manuscript was written about the same time as Sinaiticus, the fourth century A.D.
- Codex Ephraemi is an incomplete copy of the Greek Bible. It dates from the fifth century.
- Codex Bezae is named for the German reformer Theodor Beza, who presented it to the University of Cambridge in 1581. It was written in the fifth or sixth century, and contains the Gospels and Acts in Greek and Latin.

These manuscripts are all centuries older than those available to Erasmus and those who produced the *textus receptus*. As a result, translations that use these discoveries can get much closer to the original documents. Therefore, modern translations have multiplied as such manuscripts have become available to scholars.

In addition, translations today serve various audiences and needs. Some are more literal, seeking to reproduce exactly what was written by the biblical authors. The New American Standard Version and its ancestor, the American Standard Version, are examples of this type. The English Standard Version is the latest translation produced for this purpose.

Paraphrases stand at the opposite end of the translation spectrum. They attempt to reproduce the sense of the biblical text in the language and thought patterns of our day. The Living Bible was the first popular example of this approach; the New Living Bible continues its legacy. The Message is the newest version of this kind of translation.

"Dynamic equivalence" translations seek to render the Bible literally where possible but make adjustments for idioms and figures of speech where necessary. The New International Version is the most popular translation in this category. The New Revised Standard Version stands halfway between this approach and the literal. The New English Bible and its descendant, the Revised English Bible, stand between the dynamic equivalence theory and the paraphrase.

So we have a variety of translations today, not because we do not have a Bible we can trust, but because we do. Each version builds on the same reliable biblical text produced by scholars, to meet the needs of its intended audience.

What Questions Remain?

While textual critics have produced biblical texts that are more trustworthy than any other ancient document in the world, there are still passages for which scholars have not settled unanimously on the best reading. Do they affect our commitment to biblical authority? Absolutely not.

The vast majority of unresolved issues relate to inconsequential matters of spelling and grammar. Only a small number affect the meaning of a particular passage. Not one of these change any doctrine or faith practice.

Let's look at two of the most substantial passages still in question. The well-known story of the woman caught in adultery is reproduced in the New International Version with this note: "The earliest manuscripts and many other ancient witnesses do not have John 7:53–8:11." Other modern translations carry similar notations with regard to this passage. The reason is simple. This story is not found in any reliable, early Greek New Testament document.

The earliest manuscript containing it is Codex Bezae, dated to the fifth or sixth century. The few New Testament copies that used the story incorporated it at various places within John's Gospel, and many marked it with a symbol to note that its inclusion was questionable. The Greek of the story differs markedly from the rest of the Fourth Gospel, and the story interrupts the sequence of John 7:52 and 8:12. No Greek church father for a thousand years after Christ referred to the story, even those who dealt with the entire Gospel verse by verse. So New Testament scholar Bruce Metzger concludes, "the case against its being of Johannine authorship appears to be conclusive."[10]

Why do we have it in our Bibles at all? Because it was part of the *textus receptus*, the basis for the King James Verson. The translators of the King James Version included it in their Gospel of John, giving it entrance to Bible editions ever since.

Here's the point: omitting the story does not affect Christian faith or practice in any way. We know of Jesus' forgiveness and compassion from other reliable New Testament texts. The textual questions regarding John 7:53–8:11 have no bearing on the doctrines of our faith.

A second substantial passage in this regard is the ending of Mark's Gospel. Here we find the same note attached to the text: "The earliest manuscripts and some other ancient witnesses do not have Mark 16:9-20." Like John 7:53–8:11, this passage was part of the *textus receptus*, and thus was included in the King James Version.

Again, this passage is not in the earliest and best New Testament manuscripts. Church leaders Clement of Alexandria (born A.D. 150) and Origen (born A.D. 185) show no knowledge of these verses. Eusebius (born about A.D. 260) and Jerome (born A.D. 347) state that the passage was absent from almost all Greek copies of Mark known to them. The vocabulary and style of this ending are markedly different from the rest of Mark's Gospel, and the connection between verses 8 and 9 is awkward. So these verses must be considered to be later additions to the Gospel of Mark.[11]

Without Mark 16:9-20, what changes about the Christian faith? Most interpreters would answer, *Nothing*. Those who argue that baptism is essential for salvation can claim Mark 16:16; speaking in "new tongues" is mentioned in verse 17; drinking poison and handling snakes are part of verse 18. Most scholars would agree that these "signs" of salvation, found nowhere else in Scripture, were never part of Mark's original Gospel. The questions regarding baptism and "tongues" are addressed and resolved elsewhere in the New Testament.

Conclusion

So it is with the remaining textual questions of the Bible. Not one matter of doctrine, faith, or practice is at issue. Compared with other ancient books, the manuscript evidence for Scripture is overwhelmingly positive.

According to F. F. Bruce, a leading authority in this area, "The variant readings about which any doubt remains among textual critics of the New Testament affect no material question of historic fact or of Christian faith and practice."[12]

Bruce then quotes Sir Frederic Kenyon to prove his point:

> *The interval then between the dates of the original composition and the earliest extant evidence becomes so small as to be in fact negligible, and the last foundation for any doubt that the Scriptures have come down to us substantially as they were written has now been removed. Both the authenticity and the general integrity of the books of the New Testament may be regarded as finally established.*[13]

When those critical of biblical authority claim with novelist Dan Brown that "history has never had a definitive version of the book," you can know that they are wrong.[14] The Bible you have is the Bible God has preserved across thirty-five centuries. Its transmission demonstrates its divine origin and trustworthy nature. Your copy is no less authoritative than the originals. Manuscript evidence is one more reason to trust the word of God.

CHAPTER Five

The Bible Is Confirmed by External Evidence

Biblical Authority and Non-Biblical Evidence

SKEPTICS WONDER WHY WE DON'T have more positive proof of Jesus' earthly existence. Is there archaeological and non-biblical evidence to support our claim that the Bible is God's word, and that Jesus is God's Son?

Such questions appeared to be answered in part by a discovery announced in 2002 and billed as the greatest find in biblical studies since the Dead Sea Scrolls. The center of attention was a limestone ossuary (burial box or coffin). Dated by historians to the first century A.D., the box itself was not significant, as we have many such limestone boxes from the time of Jesus. What was unique was the inscription on the side: "James son of Joseph brother of Jesus."

In the first century A.D., it was typical to place the name of the deceased on the side of his burial box, and that of his father. But to identify a person by his brother was extremely unusual in the ancient world. Further, to give no clarification except the brother's name meant that the brother was noteworthy in his own right.

So it was that historians were immediately fascinated when the box came to light. Scores of books and articles were produced by scholars on both sides of the argument. Now historians have largely concluded that the inscription "brother of Jesus" is fake, added much later than the original. So we are left where we were.

But where we were is a good place to be.

Non-Christian Evidence for Jesus

The poet claims of Jesus Christ, "All the armies that have ever marched, all the navies that have ever sailed, all the parliaments that have ever sat, and all the kings that have ever reigned, put together, have not changed life on this earth as much as has that one solitary life."[1] There are more Christians on the planet than adherents of any other faith, and so the universal significance of the Christian position regarding the existence and deity of Jesus is clear. But is it justified?[2]

We believe that Jesus is Lord because the Bible teaches that it is so. But the Koran teaches that Allah is the only God. Buddhists follow their own sacred writings, as do Hindus and scores of other religions. Do we have any other evidence to support our commitment to Christ as the King of Kings? How do we refute the claim that the divinity of Jesus was a doctrine that evolved centuries after his life and death?

Before we formulate our answer, let's remember some facts about non-Christian evidences for Jesus:

- The availability of international news in Jesus' day was limited, making knowledge of his Palestinian life and work improbable for historians writing in Rome.
- Little of the literature of Jesus' era has survived (see chapter four). So we should not be surprised that non-biblical records regarding Jesus' life are limited.
- From the time of Constantine (A.D. 312), the church possessed state authority to suppress all anti-Christian literature. It considered pagan references to Jesus to be blasphemous and disposed of many of them.

- The character of the events concerning Jesus' earthly life, centering in a minor nation and religion, would have been of little interest to Rome.
- Pagan sources would have been influenced by anti-Christian rhetoric.
- The Jewish documents from the era are problematic in reliability and interpretation.

Despite these facts, historical evidence for Jesus' life, death, and resurrection is extremely helpful in confirming the authority of God's word.

Gentile references to Jesus

We'll begin with Roman historians who mention Jesus in some way. Thallus the Samaritan wrote a history of Greece and its relations with Asia from the Trojan War to his own day. It does not exist today. A Christian writer, Julius Africanus (about A.D. 180–250), referred to Thallus's history, which may have been written as early as A.D. 52. Julius Africanus stated that Thallus explained away the darkness at Jesus' crucifixion as an eclipse of the sun.[3] Julius and Eusebius believed that Thallus referenced Jesus' crucifixion. This may be the earliest pagan reference to Jesus, showing that the passion story was known in non-Christian circles in the mid-first century. Too, Thallus's statement demonstrates that the enemies of Christianity tried to refute its claims through naturalistic interpretation of the facts it reported.

Pliny the Younger was a Roman administrator who served as governor of Bithynia in Asia Minor. The nephew and adopted son of a natural historian known as Pliny the Elder, he was a great letter-writer and observer of his day. Ten books of Pliny's correspondence exist today. Pliny wrote the first Latin passage in which Jesus is mentioned. The tenth of his correspondence books, composed around A.D. 112, contains numerous letters to Emperor Trajan regarding the administration of Bithynia. One of them concerns the problem of dealing with Christians. In it he described his efforts to secure their revocation of Christ, and tells of the strange beliefs they held concerning Christ. Part of that description: "They were in the habit of meeting on a certain fixed day before it was light, where they sang in alternate verses a hymn to Christ as to a god."[4]

Pliny provides the earliest non-biblical description of Christian worship in existence today. It demonstrates that from the first generation of their movement, Christians considered Jesus to be divine. His divinity was not the result of Constantine's edicts two centuries later or an evolution in belief over several generations. Rather, believers have always known that Jesus existed, and that he was their Lord.

Tacitus (about A.D. 55–120) was the greatest historian of ancient Rome. One of his works was the *Annals* (probably eighteen books, covering the period from Augustus's death in A.D. 14 to that of Nero in A.D. 68). In *Annals* 15:44 we find the only explicit early pagan reference to Christ. Regarding the great fire in Rome during the reign of Nero, Tacitus reports:

> *Consequently, to get rid of the report [that he started the fire], Nero fastened the guilt and inflicted the most exquisite tortures on a class hated for their abominations, called Christians by the populace. Christus, from whom the name had its origin, suffered the extreme penalty during the reign of Tiberius at the hands of one of our procurators, Pontius Pilatus, and a most mischievous superstition . . . broke out.*

Tacitus was not an eyewitness to these events. But he reported them as facts of history, documenting that Jesus existed, that Jesus was crucified under Pontius Pilate, and that after Jesus' death a "superstition" resulted. "Superstition" points to something supernatural, not a normal historical occurrence. This event was the resurrection. So by A.D. 115 we have evidence for Jesus' existence and death, and the belief of his followers that he was raised from the dead.

Gaius Suetonius Tranquillas (about A.D. 65–135) was chief secretary of Emperor Hadrian (A.D. 117–38). As a Roman historian with access to the imperial records, his narratives are especially noteworthy. Suetonius reports that during Nero's reign, "Punishments were also inflicted on the Christians, a sect professing a new and mischievous religious belief" (*Nero* 16:2). Then, during the reign of Claudius, "Because the Jews at Rome caused continuous disturbances at the instigation of Chrestus, he expelled them from the city" (*Claudius* 25:4). This expulsion occurred in A.D. 49 and was recorded in Acts 18:2.

In conclusion, the Gentile evidences for Jesus make it clear that Christianity was known and reported by Rome in the first century after his death and resurrection. They also demonstrate the following:

- Jesus existed as a figure of history.
- The Christians believed in his resurrection.
- They worshiped him as their living Lord.

Jewish references to Jesus

The most significant Jewish historian of the ancient world was Flavius Josephus (about A.D. 37–97). Born in Jerusalem, Josephus belonged to an eminent priestly family and received extensive education. At the age of nineteen, he joined the Pharisees. He was opposed to Rome during the Jewish Revolt that began in A.D. 66, but he later served commander Vespasian in Jerusalem.

After the destruction of the Jewish temple in A.D. 70, Josephus moved to Rome. There he became the court historian for Emperor Vespasian. Among the works of Josephus are *History of the Jewish War*; *Antiquities*; *Autobiography*; and *On the Antiquity of the Jews*.

In *Antiquities*, Jesus is mentioned twice. The first reference: Ananias "called a Sanhedrin together, brought before it James, the brother of Jesus who was called the Christ, and certain others . . . and he delivered them to be stoned" (*Antiquities* 20:9:1). Note that Josephus mentions Jesus without comment or clarification, possibly depending on his previous statement in *Antiquities* 18:3:3 regarding Jesus (see the next reference, the *Testimonium Flavianum*). If so, this passage in *Antiquities* 20:9:1 verifies the previous text's basic authenticity. Too, it shows us Jesus' importance, since he could be identified by name alone.

The reference in *Antiquities* 18:3:3, sometimes called the *Testimonium Flavianum*, states:

> *Now, there was about this time, Jesus, a wise man, if it be lawful to call him a man, for he was a doer of wonderful works, a teacher of such men as receive the truth with pleasure. He drew over to him both many of the Jews, and many of the Gentiles. He was Christ; and when Pilate, at the suggestion of the principal men amongst us, had condemned him to the cross, those that loved him at the first did not forsake him, for he appeared to them alive again the third day, as the divine prophets had foretold these and ten thousand other wonderful things concerning him; and the tribe of Christians, so named from him, are not extinct at this day.*

If this reference is authentic, it would provide an extremely significant attribution of divinity and resurrection to Jesus. Since Josephus would have first-hand information, his statement would be especially important.

However, most interpreters do not believe that the uniquely Christian elements of the text came from Josephus. Rather, they affirm that the basic facts of the *Testimonium Flavianum* may be accepted as genuine, with theological interpretations held in judgment. As such, the text is an important Jewish record of the basic facts of Christ's life, death, and reported resurrection.

The Talmud tradition provides additional Jewish attestation to Jesus' existence. The Talmud was a compilation of Jewish oral traditions completed around A.D. 200. The written record of the oral tradition is known as the Mishnah. Ancient commentary on it was called the Gemara. The combination of the Mishnah and the Gemara is the Talmud.

We would expect the Talmud to be biased against Jesus. We would be correct.

It is noteworthy that those who composed these early rejections of Jesus as Messiah never thought to deny his existence. This would have been the easiest way to debunk the growing Christian movement. But these writers, working so close to the time of Jesus' earthly ministry, knew that such claims would be rejected. So even their anti-Christian rhetoric further makes the case for Jesus' historical existence.

Early Christian Records

The earliest Christian writers produced volumes of important works on the life and significance of Jesus. Many of these writings contain vital facts regarding the Christ event. We would expect these materials to report positively on the Christian faith they reflect. The point is that these faith commitments were made at a very early time in Christian history, not as the product of generations of evolution and political manipulation.

- Clement of Rome (A.D. 95) is generally considered to be the earliest extra-biblical Christian author. He was the leading elder at the Roman church. He wrote his *Letter to the Church at Corinth*, also known as *1 Clement*, to help settle a dispute between laity and elders within the Corinth congregation. His letter sets out the divinity of Christ and Christ's delegation of authority to his apostles. Clement anchors the authority of the gospel in the resurrection of Christ.
- Ignatius (about A.D. 110) composed seven letters to six churches and one individual (Polycarp). Polycarp was on his way to execution in Rome. The letter of Ignatius to the Trallians documents Jesus' lineage, life, crucifixion, and resurrection. His epistle to the Smyrneans affirms Jesus' lineage and virgin birth, baptism, crucifixion, and resurrection. His letter to the Magnesians affirms the fact of Jesus' birth, death, and resurrection.
- Quadratus (about A.D. 125) provided an early apologetic for the historicity of Jesus' miracles.
- *The Letter of Barnabas* (about 100–130) shows that Jesus fulfilled the Old Testament laws.

- Justin the Martyr (about A.D. 100–165) provides significant and lengthy treatments of Jesus' historicity. *First Apology* documents Jesus' life, death, and resurrection.

These and other early Christian documents demonstrate the historicity of Jesus' earthly life and work. They were written at a time when such claims could be countered easily if they were fictitious. These early Christian letters reproduce much of the New Testament, and they provide independent evidence for its trustworthiness and authority.

So, on the basis of non-biblical evidences, we can know that:

- Jesus Christ existed.
- He was crucified by Pontius Pilate.
- The first Christians believed Jesus to be raised from the dead.
- The early church worshiped Jesus as Lord and God.
- Jewish opponents tried to slander Jesus but never to deny his existence.
- The facts of Christian faith were set forth early in church history and are no invention of later revisionists.

The Roman Empire persecuted Christians because they claimed no King but the Lord Jesus. Their radical faith and courage, and the rapid spread of their movement, have no other explanation except that the living Christ changed their lives and empowered their faith. Multiplied thousands died because of their commitment to Jesus.

Extra-biblical evidences thus demonstrate the trustworthiness of Scripture's central claim: *Jesus is Lord.* Such historicity is excellent evidence for the authority of the Book that records his life and ministry.

Archaeological Evidence for the Bible

Not only do we have outstanding non-biblical evidences to substantiate the central theme of Scripture, we also have excellent archaeological data to support the rest of the biblical witness. Here are just a few examples, listed in the order of their biblical occurrence.[5]

Old Testament discoveries

In 1993, Israeli archaeologists were sifting through debris as they worked on the ruins of the ancient city of Dan in upper Galilee. They discovered an inscription, part of a shattered "stele" (monument) and dated to the ninth century before Christ. It commemorated a military victory by the king of Damascus over the king of Israel and the house of David. It cited the "House of David" clearly.[6]

Archaeologists have also discovered dramatic evidence of Solomon's amazing wealth and building campaigns. Excavations at Hazor, Megiddo, and Gezer provide insights concerning the time of Solomon's reign. Part of the temple Solomon built still stands on the eastern side of the temple mount.[7]

Babylonian chronicles of the destruction of Jerusalem parallel the biblical records of this tragic event.[8] Also, ruins of Nebuchadnezzar's palace complex have been discovered, proving his existence and significant role in the ancient Middle East.[9]

New Testament evidences

According to Luke 3:1, Lysanias was tetrarch of Abilene during the beginning of John the Baptist's ministry. But no evidence of Lysanius's existence had been discovered, until an inscription was found that records a temple dedication by him. His name, title, and place all agree with Luke's description.[10]

In 1961, excavations at the seaside ruins of Caesarea Maritima unearthed a first-century inscription. Badly damaged, the Latin inscription reads in part, *Tiberieum . . . [Pon]tius Pilatus . . . [Praef]ectus Juda[ea]e.* The inscription confirms the status of Pontius Pilate as the prefect or governor of Judea.[11]

Yhohnn Yehohanan was a crucifixion victim, executed during the Jewish Revolt in A.D. 70. In 1968, his remains were discovered. His legs were fractured, evidence of the typical Roman means by which death was hastened. Nails were driven through his wrists and heels.[12] His death corresponds precisely with the descriptions of Jesus' crucifixions found in the Gospels (see John 19:17–32).

Luke describes Paul's ministry in Corinth and this attack: "While Gallio was proconsul of Achaia, the Jews made a united attack on Paul" (Acts 18:12). Gallio ejected Paul's accusers from his court (Acts 18:16) and refused to prosecute Paul. Critics were skeptical of Luke's claim that Gallio was "proconsul" of Achaia during the time of Paul's ministry there. Then an inscription was discovered at Delphi with this exact title for Gallio; it dates him to A.D. 51, the time Paul was in Corinth.[13]

Erastus is identified in Acts 19:22 as one of Paul's co-workers who ministered at Corinth. In excavations in the area of Corinth, an inscription was found that states, "Erastus, procurator and aedile, laid this pavement at his own expense."[14]

Fulfilled Prophecy

Does the Bible fulfill its predictions? When it makes prophetic statements regarding the future, do they come to pass? As we consider evidence for biblical authority, we should spend a moment with the fascinating subject of Messianic prophecy and its fulfillment by Jesus Christ. If any book makes promises it does not keep, we are justified in dismissing the rest of its truth claims. But if a book's prophecies rendered centuries earlier are clearly fulfilled in history, we can consider the rest of its claims to be trustworthy as well.

The importance of Messianic prophecy

Jesus appealed repeatedly to Old Testament predictions regarding himself:

- At the beginning of his ministry, Jesus read a Messianic prediction from Isaiah 61. Then Jesus said to the waiting crowd, "Today this scripture is fulfilled in your hearing" (Luke 4:21).

- He told his critics, "You diligently study the Scriptures because you think that by them you possess eternal life. These are the Scriptures that testify about me, yet you refuse to come to me to have life. . . . If you believed Moses, you would believe me, for he wrote about me" (John 5:39–40, 46).
- At the Last Supper, Jesus warned his disciples, "It is written: 'And he was numbered with the transgressors'; and I tell you that this must be fulfilled in me. Yes, what is written about me is reaching its fulfillment" (Luke 22:37).
- At his arrest Jesus told the crowd, "This has all taken place that the writings of the prophets might be fulfilled" (Matthew 26:56).
- On Easter Sunday night he said to the two disciples traveling to Emmaus: "How foolish you are, and how slow of heart to believe all that the prophets have spoken! Did not the Christ have to suffer these things and then enter his glory?" Then, to explain what he meant, "beginning with Moses and all the Prophets, he explained to them what was said in all the Scriptures concerning himself" (Luke 24:25–26, 27).
- After his resurrection he said to his astonished disciples, "Everything must be fulfilled that is written about me in the Law of Moses, the Prophets and the Psalms" (Luke 24:44).

New Testament writers made the same appeal, claiming repeatedly that Jesus fulfilled the Old Testament predictions regarding the Messiah:

- At Pentecost, Peter cited prophecies from Joel 2, Psalm 16, and Psalm 110 in claiming that Jesus was the promised Messiah (Acts 2:14–36).
- Peter later explained Jesus' crucifixion to a crowd at Jerusalem: "This is how God fulfilled what he foretold through all the prophets, saying that his Christ would suffer" (Acts 3:18).

- Peter told Cornelius, "All the prophets testify about him that everyone who believes in him receives forgiveness of sins through his name" (Acts 10:43).
- When Paul came to Thessalonica, "As his custom was, Paul went into the synagogue, and on three Sabbath days he reasoned with them from the Scriptures, explaining and proving that the Christ had to suffer and rise from the dead. 'This Jesus I am proclaiming to you is the Christ,' he said" (Acts 17:2–3).
- Paul described his message as "the gospel [God] promised beforehand through his prophets in the Holy Scriptures" (Romans 1:2).
- Paul's message could be summarized: "what I received I passed on to you as of first importance: that Christ died for our sins according to the Scriptures, that he was buried, that he was raised on the third day according to the Scriptures" (1 Corinthians 15:3–4).

Clearly, if Jesus did not fulfill Old Testament predictions regarding the Messiah, both Jesus and his first followers were deceivers of the worst sort. Their movement depended entirely on the claim that Jesus was the promised Messiah of God. It still does.

Representative Messianic prophecies

More than 300 times, the Old Testament makes claims or predictions regarding the coming Messiah.[15] Jesus fulfilled every prophecy. Most scholars date Malachi, the last book of the Old Testament, at about 400 B.C., demonstrating that these predictions were not made during Jesus' day. Translators who created the Septuagint, the Greek Old Testament, began their work about 250 B.C. At the very least, therefore, there were more than two centuries between the last prediction and Jesus' fulfillment.

Listed in order relative to Jesus' earthly life, here are some of the main prophecies to consider:

- Born of a woman's seed (Genesis 3:15; Galatians 4:4)
- Born of a virgin (Isaiah 7:14; Matt. 1:18, 24–25; Luke 1:26–35)
- Descended from Abraham (Gen. 22:18; Matt. 1:1; Gal. 3:16)
- Descended from Isaac (Gen. 21:12; Luke 3:23, 34; Matt. 1:1–2)
- Descended from Jacob (Numbers 24:17; Luke 3:23, 34)
- Part of the tribe of Judah (Micah 5:2; Luke 3:23, 33; Matt. 1:1–2)
- From the family line of Jesse (Isa. 11:1; Luke 3:23, 32; Matt. 1:1, 6)
- From the house of David (Jeremiah 23:5; Luke 3:23, 31; Matt. 1:1)
- Born at Bethlehem (Mic. 5:2; Matt. 2:1)
- Presented with gifts (Psalm 72:10; Matt. 2:1, 11)
- Children would die (Jer. 31:15; Matt. 2:16)
- Would be anointed by the Spirit (Isa.11:2; Matt. 3:16–17)
- Preceded by a messenger (Isa. 40:3; Malachi 3:1; Matt. 3:1–2)
- Would minister in Galilee (Isa. 9:1; Matt. 4:12–17)
- Would perform miracles (Isa. 35:5–6; Matt. 9:35)
- Would enter Jerusalem on a donkey (Zechariah 9:9; Luke 19:35–37)
- A friend would betray him (Ps. 41:9; Matt. 10:4)
- Forsaken by his disciples (Zech. 13:7; Mark 14:50)
- Accused by false witnesses (Ps. 35:11; Matt. 26:59–60)
- Silent before his accusers (Isa. 53:7; Matt. 27:12)
- Wounded and bruised (Isa. 53:5; Matt. 27:26)
- Smitten and spat upon (Isa. 50:6; Matt. 26:67)
- Mocked (Ps. 22:7–8; Matt. 27:29)
- Hands and feet pierced (Ps. 22:16; Luke 23:33)
- Crucified with thieves (Isa. 53:12; Matt. 27:38)
- Prayed for his persecutors (Isa. 53:12; Luke 23:34)
- Friends stood afar off (Ps. 38:11; Luke 23:49)
- Garments parted and lots cast (Ps. 22:18; John 19:23–24)
- Would suffer thirst (Ps. 69:21; John 19:28)
- Gall and vinegar offered (Ps. 69:21; Matt. 27:34)
- Would be forsaken by God (Ps. 22:1; Matt. 27:46)
- Would commit himself to God (Ps. 31:5; Luke 23:46)

- No bones broken (Ps. 34:20; John 19:33)
- His side pierced (Zech. 12:10; John 19:34)
- Buried in a wealthy man's tomb (Isa. 53:9; Matt. 27:57–60)
- Would be raised from the dead (Ps. 16:10; Acts 2:31)
- Would ascend to heaven (Ps. 68:18; Acts 1:9)
- Would be seated at the right hand of God (Ps. 110:1; Hebrews 1:3)

Clearly, the Bible keeps its promises. Its central figure is who he claimed to be: the Messiah of God.

Conclusion

The archaeological and non-biblical evidences for the Son of God are exactly what we would expect to find. Roman historians took little notice of Jesus' life and death until his movement became significant to the Empire. Archaeological evidence documents the existence of the most significant kings of the Old Testament and leaders of the New. Nothing in the archaeological record contradicts Scripture. Rather, we find much outside the Bible to confirm that which we find inside its pages.

Fulfilled prophecy is yet another matter. Here we find evidence so remarkable as to be almost beyond human comprehension. Taken together, non-biblical historical records, archaeology, and fulfilled prophecy offer us yet more reasons to trust the authority of God's word today.

CHAPTER Six

The Bible Is the Book God Meant Us to Have

How the Canon Was Created

MY EARLIEST EXPERIENCE WITH THE Bible was leafing through an ancient King James Version my parents kept in the guest room. The fountain-penned family tree written in calligraphy in the first pages fascinated me. The printed *thees* and *thous* made no sense, *the begats* even less. I assumed the entire thing, in black leather, had been handed from God to human beings.

Most people know better. They've heard somewhere along the way that some books were excluded from the Bible, and they wonder why. Maybe a group of church officials decided the whole thing. Maybe there were books that told a different story than the one we have in our Bibles. Maybe there was a smoke-filled room somewhere.

One of the most common questions I'm asked about the Bible concerns the canon (from the Greek *kanon*, describing a straight rod used as a rule).[1] The word refers to the decision to limit Scripture to the sixty-six books Protestants affirm as God's word. The question about the canon was raised by the recent publishing phenomenon, *The Da Vinci Code*. In Dan Brown's bestselling novel, the "historian"

Leigh Teabing explained to the incredulous Sophie Neveu that Constantine "upgraded Jesus' status" from human to divine, and thus needed to "rewrite the history books." And so "sprang the most profound moment in Christian history" as "Constantine commissioned and financed a new Bible, which omitted those gospels that spoke of Christ's *human* traits and embellished those gospels that made Him godlike. The earlier gospels were outlawed, gathered up, and burned."[2] Thus, the novelist says, the Bible we read today was created.

The actual story is quite different.

How the Hebrew Scriptures Came to Be

Christians typically call the thirty-nine books from Genesis to Malachi the Old Testament, but those who wrote the New Testament didn't. When Paul, writing from death row in Rome, asked Timothy for his scrolls and parchments (2 Timothy 4:13), he was asking for his copies of the only Bible he knew.

Paul was asking for scrolls of the various books of Hebrew Scripture. Their order was not of practical importance, since each scroll or book was separate. Then the modern book evolved, as individual sheets of a scroll were cut apart and sewn together. Only then did the particular order of the biblical books matter.

Most scholars appropriately call these books the Hebrew Bible, in deference to the Jewish faith they express. The Hebrew Scriptures were first divided into Law, Prophets, and Writings, the arrangement current in Jesus' day. The resurrected Lord told his disciples, "Everything must be fulfilled that is written about me in the Law of Moses, the Prophets and the Psalms" (Luke 24:44). The Psalms represented the Writings.

In developing the Hebrew Bible, the Law was the first to be written and compiled. Here we find the religious regulations of the Jewish faith, including the Ten Commandments and the priestly codes for sacrifices and daily living. Stories of early Hebrew history were included as well, from the creation of the world to the journey of Israel to the edge of Canaan. The section was called *Torah*, meaning *instruction*. It was later divided into five parts, called the *Pentateuch* (meaning *five books*):

- Genesis
- Exodus
- Leviticus
- Numbers
- Deuteronomy

Next came the Prophets, called *Nebiim* by the Jews. This section included prophetic writings and also histories of their era.

The Jews arranged these writings into eight books. The first four are called the "Former Prophets":

- Joshua
- Judges
- 1 and 2 Samuel
- 1 and 2 Kings

Notice that Samuel and Kings are combined into one book, since they were believed to reflect a single author and purpose. We think of them as historical books, but they record the prophetic ministry of Jewish leaders from Joshua to the Babylonian captivity and destruction of Jerusalem (about 586 B.C.).

The last four books were called the "Latter Prophets":

- Isaiah
- Jeremiah
- Ezekiel
- "The Twelve"

These tell the story of prophets and leaders from the eighth century B.C. to near the end of the Old Testament era. The "Twelve" are our so-called "minor" prophets (given this rather unfortunate name only because they are shorter than other prophetic writings):

- Hosea
- Joel
- Amos
- Obadiah
- Jonah
- Micah
- Nahum
- Habakkuk
- Zephaniah
- Haggai
- Zechariah
- Malachi

Last came the "Writings," called *Ketubim* by the Jews. Some were compiled from earlier, smaller books (such as individual psalms). The Hebrew Bible lists eleven books in this section:

- Psalms
- Proverbs
- Job
- Song of Solomon
- Ruth
- Lamentations
- Ecclesiastes
- Esther
- Daniel
- Ezra and Nehemiah
- 1 and 2 Chronicles

As with Samuel and Kings, the books of Ezra–Nehemiah and the books of 1–2 Chronicles are each combined as one book. We think of Ezra, Nehemiah, and 1–2 Chronicles as historical literature, but they also contain spiritual guidance and wisdom.

The Hebrew Bible begins with Genesis, as does ours today. But it ends not with Malachi but 2 Chronicles.

These books were written and compiled over centuries of use. Extreme care and meticulous discipline was devoted to the work of transmitting the Hebrew Bible. Scribes devoted their entire lives to the task, and they performed with amazing skill. The "Masoretic Text" (the Hebrew Scriptures as copied by the Masoretic scribes) has been preserved with very little change from the Old Testament era to today.

When the first Dead Sea Scrolls were discovered in 1947, they gave us copies of the Old Testament nearly a thousand years older than any manuscripts we possessed to that point. They were copied by Essenes living in caves around the Dead Sea, primarily in the first century before Christ. So few changes had crept into the text over the centuries that it was clear that the Hebrew Bible has been preserved with great success.

Then, according to Jewish tradition, a council of rabbis and scholars met at Jamnia (or Jabneh) on the Mediterranean coast of western Judea, in A.D. 90 and again in A.D. 118. They responded to the destruction of the Jewish temple in A.D. 70 and the need to preserve their sacred writings. Also, the Christian Scriptures were gaining in popularity, and Jewish leaders wanted to compile their canon to prevent Christian influence.

The Jamnia councils finalized the list of books in the Hebrew Bible as we have them today, recognizing what their people had accepted as God's word for centuries. Josephus, the first-century Jewish historian, records the belief of his people regarding their Scriptures:

> *We have not an innumerable multitude of books among us, disagreeing and contradicting one another, [as the Greeks have,] but only twenty-two books, which contains the records of all past times; which are justly believed to be divine.*[3]

How the New Testament Joined the Old

Justin the Martyr was one of Christianity's first heroes. He was killed for his faith around A.D. 165, but not before producing powerful writings in defense of Christian truth. In one of his books, he provides the oldest non-biblical description of Christian worship we have:

> *On the day called Sunday, all who live in cities or in the country gather together to one place, and the memoirs of the apostles or the writings of the prophets are read, as long as time permits; then, when the reader has ceased, the president verbally instructs, and exhorts to the imitation of these good things.*[4]

The "writings of the prophets" refers to the Hebrew Bible, and "memoirs of the apostles" to our New Testament. By the mid-second century, then, the church owned a set of writings that reflected Christian theology. Why did this new set of books come to be?

Why another Testament?

The eyewitnesses to Jesus' life and ministry were dying or growing old. All the apostles except John likely died before A.D. 70. So there was an immediate need to preserve their witness and authority. Mark compiled Peter's sermons into a life of Christ, probably the first Gospel. Luke recorded Paul's life and teaching ministry to create Luke and Acts. Matthew wrote his own Gospel; John did the same.

This first-person nature of the Christian Scriptures is crucial to their authority. We do not read from accounts compiled centuries after the fact. Rather we study records produced by those who were there. Every time we open the New Testament, we step across twenty centuries into the life of Jesus and his first followers. And we learn to join them.

An additional reason for writing the New Testament is that Christian missionaries needed literature to spread the gospel. As they encountered literate peoples in the larger Roman Empire, they wanted to provide materials that would lead the lost to Christ and encourage churches in their witness. New believers and leaders needed ministry training. Their churches needed a doctrinal standard. Their people needed practical guidelines for faith and practice.

Most of all, Jesus' followers wanted to preserve Jesus' words. Their Lord wrote no books, trusting his followers to record his teachings for generations to come. The Gospels and letters of the New Testament were produced for this purpose. The first Christians knew Jesus personally as one "which we have heard, which we have seen with our eyes, which we have looked at and our hands have touched" (1 John 1:1). They wanted the entire world to have the same privilege. Every time we open the New Testament, Jesus preaches again.

Why these books?

The first step toward a canon for the Christian Scriptures came about as the result of a crisis. Around A.D. 140, a wealthy, influential church leader named Marcion came to believe that Christians should reject the entirety of the Hebrew Bible as legalism. He adopted Pauline theology so fully that he thought most of the other Christian writings should be ignored. His list of accepted books included ten of Paul's letters (he omitted 1 and 2 Timothy and Titus) and a copy of Luke's Gospel that he edited to reflect Pauline emphases.

Church leaders acted quickly to affirm all four Gospels, and all of Paul's letters. But the crisis showed the need for the church to make a more formal list of accepted Christian Scriptures. Over time, four criteria were developed for accepting a book as inspired.

First, the book must have been written by an apostle or based on his eyewitness testimony. Gnostic writings were gaining more and more attention at this time. Gnosticism reflected a heretical theology that separated the body from the spirit. Some of the Gnostic "gospels" were purported to be written by apostles such as Thomas and Peter. In response, church leaders quickly adopted the position that a canonical book must be the clear product of an actual apostle, or based on his eyewitness accounts.

Matthew was a disciple of Jesus before he wrote his Gospel, as was John. Mark was an early missionary associate of Paul (Acts 13:4–5) and was a spiritual son to Peter (1 Peter 5:13). Early Christians believed that Mark wrote his Gospel based on the sermons and experiences Peter related to him.

Luke was a Gentile physician who likely joined Paul's second missionary journey at Troas (note Acts 16:10, where the pronoun in the narrative changes from "they" to "we"). Luke wrote his Gospel and the Book of Acts based on the eyewitness testimony of others (Luke 1:1–4). Paul's letters came from an eyewitness to the risen Christ (see Acts 9:1–6), as did the works of James (half-brother of Jesus), Peter, Jude (another half-brother of Jesus), and John.

This criteria alone excluded most of the books suggested for the canon. For instance, Clement of Rome was not an eyewitness of the Lord. Even though Clement's letter to the church at Corinth was highly respected, it was not included in the New Testament.

A *second* criteria was that the book must possess merit and authority in its use. Here it was easy to separate those writings that were inspired from those that were not. For instance, an ancient book called *The First Gospel of the Infancy of Jesus Christ* tells of a man changed into a mule by a bewitching spell but converted back to being a man when the infant Christ was put on his back for a ride (7:5–27). In the same book, the boy Jesus caused clay birds and animals to come to life (15:1–7), stretched a throne his father had made too small (16:5–16), and took the lives of boys who opposed him (19:19–24). It wasn't hard to know that such books did not come from the Holy Spirit.

Third, a book must be accepted by the larger church, not just a particular congregation. Paul's Letter to the Ephesians was an early instance of a letter that became circular in nature, that is, read by churches beyond Ephesus. His other letters soon acquired such status. In fact, Peter referred to Paul's letter as "Scripture" (2 Peter 3:16). By at least A.D. 100, Paul's works were collected together and used in worship and study by the larger church.

The gospels were a different matter. Many "life of Christ" documents began to appear in the early years of Christianity. Among them were two books on Jesus' infancy (one claiming falsely to be written by Thomas); and the *Gospel of Nicodemus* (sometimes called the *Acts of Pontius Pilate*). But none actually recorded eyewitness testimony to Jesus. They did not gain acceptance by the larger Christian movement.

By the mid-second century, only the Gospels of Matthew, Mark, Luke, and John were accepted universally, as quotations from the Christians of the era make clear. About A.D. 130, Papias referred to Mark as a "Gospel" and also mentioned Matthew and John.[5] Around 170, an Assyrian Christian named Tatian composed a "harmony" of the Gospels, using only these four. Irenaeus, bishop of Lyons in Gaul around 180, referred to the four Gospels as firmly established in the church.

The rest of the New Testament gained wide use through different processes. Acts was always considered to be part of Luke's record. Thus Acts was included immediately after the Gospels. The thirteen letters of Paul were included next, arranged from longest to shortest (not chronologically, as many assume). Hebrews was placed next, as many connected it with Paul. First Peter and 1 John were clearly written by the apostles for whom they were named.

The Greek of 2 Peter is different from that of 1 Peter, raising authorship questions for some. But then it came to be understood that 1 Peter was probably written through a secretary and 2 Peter by the apostle himself. The authorship of 2 and 3 John, James, Jude, and Revelation was eventually settled, and they were accepted and used by the larger church as well.

Fourth, a book came to be approved by the decision of church leaders. The so-called Muratorian Canon (discovered in 1740 by L. A. Muratori) was the first list to convey the larger church's opinion regarding accepted books of the New Testament canon. Compiled around A.D. 200, it represented the usage of the Roman church at the time.[6] The list does not include James, 1 and 2 Peter, 3 John, and Hebrews, since its compiler was not sure of their authorship. All were soon included in later canons.

Eusebius, the first church historian, listed in the fourth century the most widely read books in three categories: "recognized," "disputed," and "heretical." He identified as "recognized" the four Gospels, Acts, fourteen letters of Paul (Eusebius included Hebrews as Pauline), 1 John and 1 Peter, and Revelation. Among the "disputed" books, he listed as "generally accepted" James, Jude, 2 Peter, and 2 and 3 John (authorship questions remained in the minds of some). So each of the books of our New Testament had gained general acceptance by this time.

The list we have today was set forth by Athanasius, bishop of Alexandria, in his Easter letter of A.D. 367:

> *Again it is not tedious to speak of the [books] of the New Testament. These are, the four Gospels, according to Matthew, Mark, Luke, and John. Afterwards, the Acts of the Apostles and Epistles (called Catholic), seven, viz. of James, one; of Peter, two; of John, three; after these, one of Jude. In addition, there are fourteen Epistles of Paul, written in this order. The first, to the Romans; then two to the Corinthians; after these, to the Galatians; next, to the Ephesians; then to the Philippians; next to the Colossians; after these, two to the Thessalonians, and that to the Hebrews; and again, two to Timothy; one to Titus; and lastly, that to Philemon. And besides, the Revelation of John.*
>
> *These are the foundations of salvation, that they who thirst may be satisfied with the living words they contain. In these alone is proclaimed the doctrine of godliness. Let no man add to these, neither let him take ought from these.*[7]

Note that to this point, no official church council had acted on the matter of the New Testament canon. The process was *bottom up* rather than *top down*, recognizing the experiences of believers everywhere with the various books of Christian Scripture. No conspiracies or councils were involved.

Finally, the list of Athanasius was approved by church councils in A.D. 393 and 397. These councils did not impose anything new on the church. Rather, they codified what believers had already come to accept and use as the word of God. By the time the councils approved the twenty-seven books of our New Testament, they had already served as the established companion to the Hebrew Scriptures for generations.

Biblical scholar F. F. Bruce is clear: "What . . . councils did was not to impose something new upon the Christian communities but to codify what was already the general practice of these communities."[8]

Biblical commentator William Barclay agrees:

> *. . . The Bible and the books of the Bible came to be regarded as the inspired word of God, not because of any decision of any Synod or Council or Committee or Church, but because in them men found God. The supremely important thing is not what men did to these books, but what these books did to men.*[9]

So the assertion of the novelist in *The Da Vinci Code* that Constantine "created" the New Testament is patently false. Constantine had absolutely nothing to do with the formation of the biblical canon. A cursory glance at the facts exposes this allegation as anti-Christian propaganda and very poor history. The books of the New Testament we read today were compiled over centuries of use by the larger church of Jesus Christ. The God who inspired the Scriptures used his people to gather and preserve them. We have the books God intended us to possess and obey today.

What About the Apocrypha?

The word *apocrypha* means *hidden* or *obscure*. With regard to the biblical canon, the Apocrypha consists of fifteen books that some Christians accept as scriptural and others reject. Here's their story told briefly.

The apocryphal books were probably written at the end of the Old Testament era, following Malachi (about 400 B.C.). All are in Greek, although the Book of Sirach seems to have had a Hebrew original. Jews living in Alexandria, Egypt, accepted these books as part of divine revelation. Jews living in Palestine never accepted them as scriptural. All are rejected by Judaism today. Here are the books: 1 Esdras; 1 Maccabees; 2 Maccabees; Tobit; Judith; Additions to the Book of Esther; The Song of the Three Young Men; Susanna; Bel and the Dragon; The Wisdom of Solomon; Wisdom of Jesus the Son of Sirach (also known as Ecclesiasticus); Baruch; The Letter of Jeremiah; The Prayer of Manasseh; 2 Esdras.

Now the story shifts to Jewish scholars meeting in Alexandria in the second century before Christ. Their goal: to translate the Hebrew

Bible into the more-popular Greek language. The process took 200 years to complete. It produced the *Septuagint* (from the Latin word for *seventy*). According to legend, seventy Jewish scholars (it was actually seventy-two) translated the Pentateuch, the first five books of the Hebrew Bible, in seventy days. Given that they lived and worked in Alexandria, where the apocryphal books were popular, these scholars included these books in their translation, lending them credibility and authority.

Next, Jerome enters the story. The greatest Bible scholar of his day, in A.D. 382 he began translating the Bible into Latin (the "Vulgate," from the Latin word for "common"). He completed his work in 405. He initially used the Septuagint for his Old Testament translation. Thus he encountered the books of the Apocrypha. Jerome included them in his Latin Bible, which gave them entrance to the Roman Catholic Church. In 1546, the Council of Trent decreed that the Vulgate would be the official Latin Bible of the Church. So Catholics include the Apocrypha in their versions of Scripture today.

Why are these books not in Protestant Bibles? When the Protestant Reformation began nearly 500 years ago, the reformers noted that no apocryphal book is quoted specifically in the New Testament. Further, the reformers cited scholarly church fathers who maintained a sharp distinction between the Hebrew Bible and these Greek additions. They concluded that these books, while informative history and narrative, should not be considered divine revelation.

When Martin Luther translated the Bible into German, he refused to include the Apocrypha. From that time to today, Protestant Bibles do not contain the apocryphal books. Catholic translations do. Some Bible editions include them for reference purposes, but not as Holy Scripture.

As long as Protestants and Catholics disagree over the authority of the Apocrypha, the question of the canon will remain part of theological discussion. But there is no other question regarding the biblical canon. All Christians believe that we have all that God intended to preserve and transmit to his people.

Conclusion

So who decided what books should be in the Bible? Ultimately, their Author. The same Holy Spirit who inspired the biblical revelation (2 Peter 1:20–21) led the Christian movement to those books the Holy Spirit inspired. You can know that the Bible you hold today is the book God means you to have.

Biblical authority is thus enhanced by discussing the canon. Contrary to some critics, the process of compiling the books of Scripture reflects their divine origin and supernatural transmission. It is nothing less than a miracle that a process so free of centralized control could produce such a clear consensus.

New Testament scholar William Barclay speaks for a multitude of scholars on this subject: "To study the Canon of Scripture is not to come away with a lesser view of Scripture, but with a far greater view, for it is to see the unanswerable power of the word of God in action in the minds and hearts of men and women."[10]

My first assumption as a child regarding the origin of the Bible was right after all: God did "hand" the Bible to us, through us.

CHAPTER Seven
The Bible Tells of God's Miraculous Acts

Biblical Authority and Miracles

When President John Kennedy entertained a group of Nobel Prize winners in the White House in December of 1962, he welcomed them as the most distinguished gathering of talents ever assembled in the Executive Mansion, except perhaps when Thomas Jefferson dined there alone.

Jefferson was indeed a Renaissance man. Conversant in Greek as well as in English, French, Spanish, Latin, he was easily able to read the New Testament in Greek, its original language. He was fascinated with the ethical teachings of Jesus. He believed that Jesus' "system of morality was the most benevolent and sublime . . . ever taught, and consequently more perfect than those of any of the ancient philosophers."[1]

However, Jefferson mourned that the task of preserving these teachings "fell on the most unlettered and ignorant men; who wrote, too, from memory, and not till long after the transactions had passed." As a result, "the doctrines which he really delivered were defective as a whole, and fragments only of what he did deliver have come to us mutilated, misstated, and often unintelligible."[2]

The "mutilated" record of Jesus' life and work included miraculous elements that Jefferson could not reconcile with his deistic worldview. God was to Jefferson the Creator of the universe who did not meddle in the affairs of his creation. God allowed the world to function according to the natural laws he incorporated into its operations. So Jefferson considered himself "a Christian, in the only sense he [Jesus] wished any one to be; sincerely attached to his doctrines, in preference to all others; ascribing to himself every human excellence; and believing he never claimed any other."[3]

Consequently, Jefferson removed from the Gospels every reference to the miraculous, preserving only Jesus' ethical statements. The resulting "Jefferson Bible" ends thus: "There laid they Jesus, and rolled a great stone to the door of the sepulcher, and departed."[4]

Thomas Jefferson was not the first or the last to reject biblical authority because of its claims to record the miraculous. There was a time when the science and faith debate led many to believe that acceptance of miracles was intellectually naïve, if not dangerous. Now, as we'll see in more detail in the next chapter, things are a bit different. The postmodern movement has opened the door for "spirituality" of all kinds, whether it is based on miracles or not. Such claims can be "my" truth without being "your" truth.

However, I still speak often with people who struggle to reconcile scientific materialism with the biblical narratives. They do not believe people can walk on water today, and so they wonder how to accept the New Testament claim that Jesus did. They have not witnessed incontrovertible proof of divine healing, and so they struggle with biblical statements that Jesus performs such miracles.

Several years ago, I spent some extended time with a geologist who was visiting our church and considering Christianity. His great struggle was that he could not reconcile his knowledge of our planet's origins with what he had been told was the biblical account of creation. He could not trust in Christ as his Lord if he could not trust the book that revealed Christ to him.

What would you say to a person who denies the miraculous? Let's learn how the conversation helps us affirm biblical authority today.

The Importance of Miracles

C. S. Lewis defines a "miracle" as "an interference with Nature by supernatural power."[5] At the very beginning of his discussion he sets out the terms of the debate: some believe that nothing exists but nature ("naturalists"), while others believe that something besides nature exists ("supernaturalists"). The question is: which is right?[6]

From its very beginnings, the biblical worldview has argued for supernaturalism. "Signs," "wonders," and "power" are found in both the Old and New Testaments. Miraculous "signs" confirmed Moses' authority (Exodus 3:12: 4:3–8), and God's message (Judges 6:17; Isaiah 38:7; Jeremiah 44:29). "Wonders" accompanied signs (Exod. 7:3; Deuteronomy 26:8; see also Exod. 4:21). Miraculous "power" defeated the enemies of God's people (Exod. 15:6–7).

In the New Testament, Jesus' miracles were "signs" (John 2:11; 6:2; 9:16; 11:47). So also were the resurrection (Matthew 12:39–40) and the apostles' miraculous acts (Acts 2:43; 4:16, 30; 8:13; 14:3). "Wonders" describes these miraculous acts and is used with the word "signs" (John 4:48; Acts 6:8; 14:3).[7]

Jesus' ministry was validated in large part by the miracles he performed. He claimed that "the very work that the Father has given me to finish, and which I am doing, testifies that the Father has sent me" (John 5:36). Part of this "work" was "the miracles I do in my Father's name" (John 10:25).

When John the Baptist sent messengers to ask Jesus if he were really the Messiah, "at that very time Jesus cured many who had diseases, sicknesses and evil spirits, and gave sight to many who were blind. So he replied to the messengers, 'Go back and report to John what you have seen and heard: The blind receive sight, the lame walk, those who have leprosy are cured, the deaf hear, the dead are raised, and the good news is preached to the poor" (Luke 7:21–22).

Jesus appealed to his skeptics, "Do not believe me unless I do what my Father does. But if I do it, even though you do not believe me, believe the miracles, that you may know and understand that the Father is in me, and I in the Father" (John 10:37–38). He made the same appeal to his disciples: "Believe me when I say that I am in the

Father and the Father is in me; or at least believe on the evidence of the miracles themselves" (John 14:11).

Early Christians understood the significance of miracles for Jesus' divinity and his movement. Origen (about 185–254) claimed that the apostles would have gained no hearing without miracles. Justin the Martyr (executed about 165) argued for a Christ who healed the sick and raised the dead. Athanasius (about 296–373) claimed that Jesus proved his divinity by his miracles. Gregory of Nyssa (about 330–395) stated that Jesus' miracles convinced his followers of his divinity.[8]

From the New Testament to today, those who affirm the biblical worldview accept the category of the supernatural. We believe that biblical miracles were sensible events, verifiable to the eye and/or ear. They required the presence of the supernatural, not merely the improbable. Too, they were performed within a redemptive context. They were not ends in themselves, but they were intended to lead their recipients and witnesses to spiritual realities.

Without the possibility of miracles, the whole purpose of the Christian faith is defeated. The biblical worldview is not a mere life philosophy. Rather, believers are convinced that the gospel is "the power of God for the salvation of everyone who believes" (Romans 1:16). If God cannot or will not do the supernatural, no soul can be set free from hell for heaven, transformed from death to life.

Salvation is itself a miracle of the highest magnitude. If Thomas Jefferson was right and the Creator does not intervene in his creation, then "Christ has not been raised, either. And if Christ has not been raised, your faith is futile; you are still in your sins. . . . If only for this life we have hope in Christ, we are to be pitied more than all men" (1 Corinthians 15:16–17, 19).

To deny the supernatural is to deny the divine authority of Scripture and the transforming faith Scripture reveals and promotes. Nothing less than our eternal destiny is at stake.

Arguing over the Supernatural

For some fifteen centuries of the Christian era, the Western world took the category of miracles largely for granted. In the last four centuries, however, intellectual wars have raged over the issue of supernaturalism. We'll look at each of the battles in turn, listening to the critic of the supernatural and then defending the miraculous.

Miracles are impossible

The first major attack on supernaturalism would not come until the seventeenth century. Benedict de Spinoza (1632–77) argued that all of reality is embraced within a single, rational substance. His pantheism viewed God as all that is. God must be immutable—unchangeable—to be God; thus, all reality is equally immutable. An unchangeable reality must operate according to unchanging laws. But miracles change the laws of nature. Therefore, miracles cannot exist.

Spinoza's mindset is still defended by deists like Jefferson, and by materialists who deny the spiritual or divine altogether. Jefferson would say that God does not violate the laws by which God's universe operates. A materialistic atheist would say that there is no possibility of the "supernatural" within the natural. So God cannot exist. The result is the same: miracles are by definition impossible.

One response to this critique is to expose its presuppositions. If a skeptic begins by denying the ability or willingness of the Creator to intervene in his creation, of course miracles are impossible. If God does not exist, obviously God cannot do the supernatural. But such an argument does not answer the question; rather, it begs it. It is no solution to the problem to deny the existence of the problem.

The "falsification principle" of philosopher Antony Flew (1923–) is worth considering in this regard. Flew claimed that Christianity is irrational, since nothing can falsify its beliefs. According to his critique, Christians will allow no evidence or logic to refute their faith.[9] Of course, Paul identified the ultimate falsification of the Christian movement: "if Christ has not been raised, our preaching is useless and so is your faith" (1 Corinthians 15:14).

It seems to me that Flew's thesis is more damaging to materialism than to supernaturalism. The skeptic who begins his argument by the *de facto* denial of the supernatural cannot allow any evidence to count against his presupposition. If Jesus could not be raised from the dead, for instance, all arguments citing the empty tomb and changed lives of the disciples are of no avail. A person who can admit no criteria by which his or her position can be refuted is not defending a rational argument but merely an opinion.

Miracles are implausible

David Hume, the eighteenth-century Scottish philosopher known to history as the "father of skepticism," was especially skeptical about miracles. His work on the subject made clear his doubts.

Hume was willing to admit the plausibility of a miracle, if those who claim to witness it meet certain criteria.[10] Those who claim to have seen the miraculous must be:

- Numerous. The more who see the miracle, the more likely their testimony. A hermit living in a mountain cave who witnesses a UFO is less believable than a crowd who sees the same phenomenon.
- Intelligent. A person of limited intellect might struggle to understand the "miracle" that I can type on this box and produce printed documents.
- Educated. To those who have never learned about airplanes, one flying overhead is a miracle of the highest significance.
- Of unquestioned integrity. The person selling an encounter with an alien is less credible than one with nothing to profit.
- Willing to undergo severe loss if wrong. The more insistent and sacrificial the witness, the more likely his or her story.
- In a region of the world where the story can be validated. Actually being able to go to the location is important.

Hume believed that no eyewitness to the miraculous could withstand such scrutiny. Of course, he was wrong. Those who witnessed the resurrected Christ meet each of Hume's criteria:

- Numerous. More than 500 saw the risen Lord (1 Cor. 15:6).
- Intelligent. Several of the apostles owned and operated a fishing business (Luke 5:1–11). Another was a tax-collector, a demanding intellectual profession (Matt. 9:9). Paul was one of the most brilliant scholars of his day.
- Educated. Paul was trained by Gamaliel (Acts 22:3), a man of "great learning" (Acts 26:24). The other disciples were schooled in the Scriptures, able to quote them from memory. The Sanhedrin's assessment that the disciples were "unschooled, ordinary men" (Acts 4:13) meant only that they had not attended rabbinic schools.
- Of unquestioned integrity. Of all the criticisms brought against Christians in the Book of Acts, no skeptic thought to attack their character. They were known even to their enemies to be people of honesty.
- Willing to undergo severe loss. All but John were martyred, and he was exiled on the prison island of Patmos.
- Able to be validated. Joseph of Arimathea's empty tomb was available to any who wished to see it. Paul could say of Agrippa, "The king is familiar with these things, and I can speak freely to him. I am convinced that none of this has escaped his notice, because it was not done in a corner" (Acts 26:26).

Miracles are implausible only to those whose presuppositions render them so. If, on the other hand, the Creator of the earth is also a loving Father to its residents, he will want a personal relationship with his children. No father can watch his family impassively as a clockmaker watches his invention run down. He will intervene in their lives often.

If there is a personal God who desires relationship with us, deistic naturalism is far less plausible than supernaturalism.

Accepting miracles would cause us to abandon science

Science operates according to certain empirical laws. The scientific method begins with a theory, which is then tested. If the data support the theory, the experiment is repeated. Only if repeatable evidence supports the theory, is it considered valid.

Miracles are by definition not subject to this method. A woman in the first church I served as pastor was told she had pancreatic cancer and given three months to live. We prayed fervently for her. The next week she returned to her doctor, who could find no evidence of the malignancy. We believed that God worked a miracle. A scientist would need to repeat the conditions that led to this occurrence before making such a judgment. Because miracles are not testable and repeatable, they are not "scientific."

As a result, some believe they cannot admit the possibility of the miraculous and remain true to the scientific worldview. But such a conclusion is hardly warranted. No relationship can be verified by a test tube, especially a personal relationship with the God of the universe. A physicist can no more test and verify her husband's love for her children than she can her heavenly Father's love for his.

A woman once told me that she would come to my church if I could prove that God loves us. I asked her to prove that her husband loves her. She smiled and said, "He tells me that he does." I told her that he could be lying. She described loving things he did for her. I replied that he could be manipulating and misleading her. Finally she said, "You'd have to be part of my family to understand." I said, "You'd have to be part of my Father's family to understand as well."

Miracles must be seen within the Christian context if they are to be given a fair hearing. Those who deny the miraculous by definition have obviously disqualified themselves as interpreters of claims to the miraculous. Science and history are treatments of the natural order. The *super*natural is by definition beyond their realm of investigation.

Miracles are an outdated concept

Still other skeptics argue that miracles are leftover vestiges of an earlier era. Those who accept this argument make strange bedfellows, indeed.

Ludwig Feuerbach and Karl Marx, proponents of atheistic materialism, taught that miracles are supernaturalistic wishes and nothing more. Since religion is, as Marx called it, "the opiate of the people," its claim to perform miracles is a means of subjugating its believers. Those who hold onto the possibility of miracles are superstitious and naïve.

Bible interpreters who are dispensationalists argue that miracles are outdated, but for completely different reasons. This theological method divides biblical history into different "dispensations," periods of time in which God dealt with humanity in ways appropriate to that era. In this view, miracles ended with the early church. We now live in a post-apostolic era in which miracles are no longer necessary.

Some Calvinists share this rejection of miracles, but for another reason. Miracles were needed to establish the truth of Christian revelation, but they are no longer needed today. In fact, according to this view, miracles diminish the glory of God by suggesting that God must intervene in God's imperfect creation.

Rudolf Bultmann, one of the most famous New Testament scholars of the twentieth century, argued that miracles are outdated for yet a fourth reason. In his view, miracles are part of the first-century, pre-scientific worldview. As such, they act as stumbling blocks to the scientific age we are called to reach with the gospel. So we need to reinterpret them spiritually, removing them as objections to faith.

Bultmann was clear: "Man's knowledge and mastery of the world have advanced to such an extent through science and technology that it is no longer possible for anyone seriously to hold the New Testament view of the world."[11] We know that people do not "descend into hell" or "ascend into heaven." This three-tiered view of the universe must be replaced with the scientific model espoused today.

To remove these mythological problems, Bultmann proposed that we "demythologize" the biblical text. Jesus' walking on water is the victory of faith over the storms of doubt. Easter is the resurrection of faith in the disciples. By this approach we do not invalidate the gospel; rather, we communicate it effectively to a new era.

Of course, Feuerbach and Marx denied the existence of the supernatural by definition. Their approach begs the question, and has already been discussed. Dispensational and Calvinist theologians cannot cite adequate scriptural support for their rejection of contemporary miracles. Their position is the logical conclusion of their presuppositions rather than being a biblical argument. It would be wrong for God to intervene in God's creation only if God told us that God would not. In fact, God assures us of just the opposite. If the Son could become human, the most complete insertion of divinity into humanity, any other supernatural act by his Father is possible.

Bultmann's program is not as attractive to scholars as it was a generation ago. We now know that the miraculous elements of the biblical worldview are foundational to its claims. We cannot spiritualize the historical elements of the story without losing all foundation in fact and experience. And without its historical foundations, a faith that worships One "which we have seen with our eyes, which we have looked at and our hands have touched" (1 John 1:1) cannot stand.

In fact, changes in the scientific worldview over the last half-century have brought about a remarkable change in the way many scientists view the supernatural. Newtonian physics sought to explain the universe in terms of predictable mechanical causality. According to this approach, the world operates by "laws" that cannot be broken; hence miracles cannot occur.

But with Einstein's theory of relativity, these "laws" are considerably less binding on scientific exploration. Indeed, there has occurred a "radical reorientation in knowledge in which structure and matter, form and being are inseparably fused together, spelling the end of the analytical era in science."[12]

Paradox is now a reality in scientific theory. For instance, physicists still debate the means by which light travels—particle or wave? A college science major attending one of my classes at Southwestern Seminary told us that in his lab the professor said humorously, "Light travels as particle on Monday, Wednesday, and Friday. It travels as wave on Tuesday, Thursday, and Saturday. On Sunday it can do whatever it likes."

Albert Einstein himself concluded, "You will find it surprising that I think of the comprehensibility of the world . . . as a miracle."[13] He was right again.

Where You Get On Is Where You Get Off

The debate over miracles reduces to presuppositions. If we assume that God does not exist, or is an impersonal entity, or cannot or will not intervene in his creation, we have ruled out the possibility of the miraculous. If we assume that God does exist, that God is personal, and that God can and will intervene in the creation he owns, we have accepted the possibility of miracles. Which presupposition is more credible?

I would of course argue for supernaturalism, but not just because of my own experience with a personal, active God. You may well consider my experience to be misguided, manipulated, or misinterpreted. But consider the following objective facts.

One: those who have never experienced miracles are by definition unqualified to pass judgment on their existence or nature. Miracles, like all experiences, are most credible to those who encounter them firsthand. It is impossible for a blind person to experience "red." We can explain light all morning long, but the person may continue to reject the existence of color.

Thomas Sherlock made a similar point nearly two centuries ago. In arguing for the miraculous, he asked whether it would be legitimate for anyone living in a warm climate to believe in the existence of ice.[14] Growing up in Houston, Texas, my personal experience would require me to reject completely the possibility of an ice storm. In this light, a spiritual skeptic is less qualified to discuss the miraculous than one who has experienced personally the supernatural God.

Two: miracles are more probable than improbable. Science works with probabilities, not absolute certainties. Parallel lines never intersect, we're told; but we'd have to draw them forever to prove the assertion. Scientists must content themselves with probabilities. So let's ask: is it more or less probable that something miraculous sparked the Christian movement? Is it likely that people who were too afraid of the authorities to stand at Jesus' cross would soon die on their own rather than abandon their belief in his resurrection? that a scattered, frightened group of fugitives would lead a movement that would replace the Roman Empire as the dominant force in the Western hemisphere? Is it more probable that this movement is founded on the lie that Jesus rose from the dead, or on the truth of his resurrection and divinity?

Three: miracles are part of that dimension of experience that is not susceptible to scientific verification. Scientists limit themselves to the proper method for the subject to be investigated. Test tubes work in chemistry, not in quantum physics.

In the same way, it is important for us to use the proper tools in discussing the supernatural. In this regard, Ian Ramsey, a philosopher of language, makes a helpful distinction between the "first order" and "second order" of divine activity in the world.[15] In the "first order," God is generally active in the universe. Here God operates according to natural, physical laws. The language of science is appropriate for describing and investigating the results of God's creative activity.

In the "second order," God operates personally within his creation. Here God's activity by definition is not subject to the natural laws that typically govern God's universe. Since science can work only within these laws, it is unable to comprehend divine activity that transcends them.

Such inability is not the fault of science but rather is a result of its assigned field of study. We don't criticize a poet when his or her descriptions violate accepted laws of physical reality. We don't reject the laws of physics because they are unable to predict the behavior of people in love. Science and faith are no more at odds than geography and landscape art. Both describe the world from their own perspective. Neither is subject to the limitations of the other.

Conclusion

J. B. Phillip's classic call to faith, *Your God Is Too Small,* traces some of the most popular pictures of God today: a resident policeman, passing out tickets to unsuspecting motorists; a "parental hangover" from our days as children; a "grand old man" who has little to do with his grandchildren; a "meek-and-mild" Jesus who would never judge or condemn us; and "God-in-a-box," limited to our understanding and experience.

Phillips concludes his argument for the miraculous God of Scripture as follows: "Critics often complain that if the world is in its present state after nineteen centuries of Christianity, then it cannot be a very good religion." He points out that Christianity has never been in a position to control the "state of the world." Then he makes an assertion especially appropriate to our subject:

> *They misunderstand the nature of Christianity. It is not to be judged by its success or failure to reform the world which rejects it. If it failed where it is accepted there might be grounds for complaint, but it does not so fail. It is a revelation of the true way of living, the way to know God, the way to live life of eternal quality, and is not to be regarded as a handy social instrument for reducing juvenile delinquency or the divorce rate. . . . The religion of Jesus Christ changes people (if they are willing to pay the price of being changed) so that they quite naturally and normally live as "sons and daughters of God," and of course they exert an excellent influence on the community. But if real Christianity fails, it fails for the same reasons that Christ failed—and any condemnation rightly falls on the world which rejects both Him and it.*[16]

The miraculous nature of the Christian faith is not to be judged by those who reject its message and power. In fact, they are in the worst possible position to render an appropriate verdict. Those who have experienced personally the miraculous God know that God's word changes lives. They know that they can trust the authority of the Scriptures, for they have met their Author. They say with the blind man, "One thing I do know. I was blind but now I see!" (John 9:25).

CHAPTER Eight
The Bible Is an Attractive Book

Biblical Authority and the Postmodern Challenge

WE WANTED TO SEE FOR ourselves. For years I'd read and heard about "postmodernism," a different way of seeing truth and life. Scholars and commentators on culture claimed that this paradigm shift is leading to a worldview that renders our commitment to biblical authority obsolete. But I wasn't sure this shift was as threatening as all that.

So I arranged to send a film crew to interview some people in our city. Park Cities Baptist Church is located in Dallas, within easy driving distance of the West End. This is the cultural center of our city, where museums, restaurants, clubs, and nightclubs abound. Our film crew told people they were making a documentary about religion in America, but they did not tell them they were from a church. They asked people on the street what they thought about religion, good or bad.

The result was some of the most discouraging footage I've ever seen. Time after time, people called the church irrelevant and outdated. Some said we were 100 years behind the times. We were told repeatedly that we had no right to force our beliefs on anyone else, that people are entitled to their own opinions and morals. Although hardly anyone we interviewed attended church, nearly every person was sure that he or she was right: religion has to change with the times.

Of all the challenges to biblical authority we'll consider in this book, the movement called "postmodernism" is the most urgent. For reasons we'll discover in this chapter, most of the people we are trying to reach with the gospel do not believe truth is objective. They do not consider the Bible to be authoritative or its teachings mandatory. They see Christianity as *our* truth, but not necessarily *theirs*. They don't believe that biblical standards on ethical subjects are objectively relevant.

We can cite the arguments for biblical authority we've surveyed so far, building an argument from manuscripts, archaeology, and historical evidences. But many will shrug their shoulders and say, *So what?* How do we respond to this change in truth itself? How can we promote biblical authority in a day when authority itself is questioned?

From Divine to Human Knowledge

For hundreds of years, most of the Western world took for granted the idea that truth is objective. As we discovered in chapter two, the medieval world viewed the church as God's authority on earth. Church teachings and tradition governed the affairs of daily life. Church leaders chose and controlled secular authorities. *The church teaches* is all most people needed to know.

The Reformation shifted authority from church to Scripture. *The Bible teaches* became the basis for faith and practice. There was still universal agreement that truth is objective, although Catholics and Protestants differed in determining how such truth was to be determined.

In the post-World War II era when Baptists grew most rapidly, this view of authority still prevailed. Few people questioned whether biblical truth was objectively right or wrong. Moral standards were accepted, whether or not they were practiced. Whether we obeyed the teachings of the Bible or not, we knew that we should. But such a worldview has largely been replaced by one that rejects completely the last sentence. How and why?

The Reformation was not the only earthquake of its era. While Protestants and Catholics were locked in a monumental conflict between two authority structures, similar tremors were sending shock waves of a very different sort—dealing not with spiritual truth but with the way we know truth itself. Their waves have still not stopped shaking our cultural foundations.

The following diagram may help you visualize two centuries that changed everything:

Rationalism	Empiricism
Truth comes from your mind.	Truth comes from your senses.

Synthesis

Truth comes from your sense impressions,
as interpreted by your mind

Now let's see, very briefly, where these ideas came from and why they still matter.

Rationalism: trust only what you cannot doubt

Rene Descartes (1596–1650) was a very sincere Catholic and a mathematical genius. (You may remember something of "Cartesian" geometry from high school.) He wanted a way to show that his faith was as rational and logical as his mathematical knowledge. Mathematicians work with the principle of doubt. They refuse to accept their conclusions to be true until they have tested them logically and empirically.

Descartes took the same approach to the rest of his knowledge and experience. The trouble was, he soon discovered that he could doubt everything. He could doubt that he was awake and not dreaming, that he was alive and not dead. In fact, he could doubt even his own existence. The one fact he could not doubt was that he was doubting. If he was doubting, he must be thinking. He could not be thinking unless he existed. The existence of the thinking self was the first truth that doubts could not deny. Hence one of the more famous sayings in history: *cogito, ergo sum* ("I think, therefore I am").

From this foundation, Descartes worked out a very elaborate epistemology (a theory that explains how we derive our knowledge).[1] That is, what matters to us is this idea: we should trust only what we cannot doubt.

Rationalism means that truth comes from reason. However, rationalism has a fatal flaw, one you may already have noticed. If all knowledge comes from the mind, where do the senses fit in? How does the mind get data with which to work? Descartes thought that we were born with innate ideas, like our instincts. But he never solved this dilemma to everyone's satisfaction. Hence the second part of the story.

Empiricism: trust only what your senses tell you

The rationalist worldview evoked a strong reaction by those known as *empiricists*. These thinkers were convinced that our personal experiences, not our unaided human reason, are the basis for knowledge. John Locke (1632–1704) believed that the mind is born not with innate ideas (Descartes's position) but as a blank slate (*tabula rasa*). He claimed that "all ideas come from sensation or reflection," our senses or the operation of our minds on them.[2] In other words, your senses told you everything you know.

David Hume (1711–1776) took Locke's ideas even further. He claimed that no knowledge is indubitable, as it is all based on our subjective personal experiences. Our minds think they find connections between causes and their effects, but we cannot prove that these connections exist.[3]

Hume's famous analogy of the billiard ball illustrates his point. We watch the cue ball strike the eight-ball and knock it into the side pocket. But can we prove that the cue ball *caused* the eight-ball to move? Perhaps magnetic forces were at work, or unseen earth tremors, or the slant of the pool table, or other unknown factors. Our minds connect the cue ball and the eight-ball, but we cannot prove beyond any doubt that this connection is true.

However, if this approach to knowledge is correct, what role does the mind play? How are reason and senses related?

Kant: trust what your mind thinks your senses say

Now we come to one of the most important figures in Western history, and one of the least known to most of us. His approach to knowledge has changed everything about how our culture sees itself, the Bible, and truth itself. It's as if we breathe the very unseen air he created. His ideas are so pervasive that we take them for granted today.

The man is Immanuel Kant (1724–1804). His idea was simple: your senses furnish the raw data that your mind organizes into knowledge.[4]

Kant discovered that your mind asks certain questions of all the data provided by your senses—how much (quantity)? what kind (quality)? in relation to what (relation)? in what movement or direction (modality)? Your mind operates like the software on your computer's hard drive. Your senses provide data as a keyboard. The resulting "knowledge" appears on the screen or printer.

Kant's view of how we derive our knowledge has been foundational for Western thinking ever since. The good news was that it moved us past the mind/sense quagmire. It clarified the way our experiences and our reason relate. The bad news was that it created another problem, one even greater for those of us who believe in biblical authority today.

Kant's system asserted that we can have certain knowledge only of the *phenomena* (those objects present to your senses). You can believe that you are looking at these words on this page, that you are holding a pen with which to take notes, etc. But you cannot be sure of the *noumena* (that which lies beyond your senses).[5] That is, you cannot be objectively certain if the ideas that your senses are conveying to your mind are true. The way you interpret your sense data is personal and individual.

This distinction would prove critical for the shift in authority we'll survey next.

The trouble with "truth"

From Kant to today, nearly everyone in the West has believed that our minds interpret our senses, resulting in "knowledge." When our minds interpret mathematical symbols, we get mathematical knowledge. When our eyes convey impressions from a sunset, we get physical knowledge. When our reason interprets the biblical words read by our eyes, we get biblical knowledge. We'd assume that everyone understands such truth to be objective and authoritative, but we'd be wrong.

Here's the problem: my mind and senses are both individual and subjective. My sense impressions may be different from yours. Too, my mind may interpret such data differently than yours does. I can call my computer keyboard "black," while you might call it "grey." Who's to decide which is right? I cannot claim objective authority for anything I "know," and neither can you. While the "modern" world (from the Reformation to the 1960s or so) believed that truth was objective, the "postmodern" world (post-1960) isn't so sure. That's the era we inhabit and are called to win to Christ.

Perhaps you've been to the Golden Gate Bridge in San Francisco. If you've lived in the area, you likely know that the bridge is built directly over the San Andreas Fault. Yet it is one of the safest places to be when an earthquake strikes. The reason is that the pillars of the bridge are driven down into bedrock and bolted there. As long as the bolts hold the pillars to the ground, the bridge will stand solid.

"Postmodern" advocates pulled the bolts holding the pillars of the "modern" world to objective truth, one by one. Let's watch their wrenches at work.

We begin with Friedrich Nietzsche (1844–1900), who blazed the trail for postmodern philosophy.[6] This critic of the Christian faith believed that the world is made up of individual fragments that our minds reconstruct into a coherent view of "reality." The "truth" that results is only a convenient fiction created by our language.[7]

For instance, there is no such thing as *leaves*, only *leafs*. How much do *leaves* weigh? What is their color? We turn the individual entity called a *leaf* into an abstract category called *leaves* that exists only in our subjective knowledge. According to Nietzsche, all universal "truth" is derived in the same way. We create abstract principles from particular experiences. But these abstract absolutes are subjective, personal, and non-binding.

In a similar fashion, Friedrich Schleiermacher (1768–1834) believed that biblical texts are not objective truth but the reflections of their authors' experiences. So in his view the Bible is a religious diary, a collection of subjective beliefs.[8] He defined religion as *a feeling of absolute dependence*, an individual experience rather than objective, universal truth. We should focus not so much on Christianity *in general* as on *your* Christian experience or mine. Abstract doctrines are secondary and less essential to faith and practice.

Such views may well be foreign and new to you.[9] You're wondering what such an academic discussion has to do with the Bible today. But whether you have ever heard of these views and the scholars who advocated them, such ideas have come to dominate your culture.

Perhaps you've traveled in Europe and seen the empty cathedrals in most of her cities. People may hold membership in a state church by virtue of their birth and baptism onto its rolls, but they seldom if ever attend its services. They do not believe church teachings to be necessary or even relevant to their lives.

Such a worldview is becoming more and more popular in America, especially in the thirty-and-under generation. Spirituality is personal and subjective. All roads lead up the same mountain. It doesn't matter what you believe as long as you're sincere and tolerant of the beliefs of others. To suggest otherwise is to promote the kind of intolerance that produced 9–11.

Everyone "knows" that truth is subjective and ethics are personal. No one has the right to force "their" truth on anyone else. Intolerance is the cardinal sin of our culture. As long as we affirm every person's right to see the world the way that person wants, all will be well.

A Christian Response

How shall we defend the objective truth claims of Christianity and relate its good news to our postmodern world? What good is our commitment to biblical authority in a culture that does not believe in authority? How can we promote the truths of Scripture in a day when "truth" is questioned?

Postmodernism and reason

First, consider a logical response. Centuries before Christ, a school of Greek philosophy known as Skeptics argued that there are no absolutes. Of this, they were absolutely certain. Their illogical worldview is behind the postmodern approach of our day and still open to the same criticism.

If no objective truth exists, how can I accept this assertion as objectively true? According to postmoderns, no statement possesses independent and objective truth. Yet this statement is itself supposed to be independently, objectively true. We are supposed to be intolerant of intolerance. However, contrary to this view, we cannot make the absolute claim that absolutes are impossible. Postmoderns cannot have it both ways.

A *second* rational response to postmodernism considers its rejection of objective ethics. Since all moral truth is considered to be purely pragmatic and contextual, no objective position can be judged or rejected by those outside its culture. If this is so, how are we to view events such as the Holocaust?

I've noticed that postmodern relativism is popular where it is convenient. People may tell me that I have no right to force my religious convictions on them. But at the same time, they will force their legal convictions on those who wish to steal their possessions or plant a virus in their computer. There are basic moral and legal standards that everyone affirms, whether they accept objective truth or not. Murder is wrong, for example. Without such basic standards, our society would quickly descend into anarchy and chaos.

And we all know it.

It makes little sense to argue objectively that objective truth does not exist, or to apply such an approach only where it is self-serving. But our culture seems to embrace such a contradictory worldview more and more each day.

Postmodernism and practical experience

If, however, our postmodern friends simply shrug their shoulders at our rational objections and say, *So what?* we can turn to a pragmatic response. Here the postmodern rejection of modernity is in our favor. The chief obstacle to faith posed by the modern, scientific era was its insistence on empirical proof and scientific verification. We were told that an assertion had to be proven either rationally or practically before it could be considered true. Such a standard undermines all relational experience, including faith.

The postmodernist rejects such a worldview. The result is a renewed interest in spirituality unprecedented in a century. While this contemporary spirituality is unfortunately embracing all alternatives, Christianity can function at least as one of the options.

When I began speaking on college campuses twenty years ago, I was typically asked to address the questions of evolution and creation, world religions, and evil and suffering. Students wanted to talk about scientific and rational objections to the Christian faith. Now it is passé to rule out the Christian faith on such grounds. My faith may or may not possess scientific, rational merit and evidential support. But these questions are secondary. *Relevance and personal authenticity are the key today.*

Students are open to Christian faith, Eastern mysticism, Judaism, and New Age spirituality. Our culture is fascinated with spiritual truth, the newer the better. How can we make an appeal for biblical authority and lifestyle in a marketplace of spiritual competitors, each of which is relatively true? We can do it by reversing the "modern" strategy. In modernity we told our culture, *Christianity is true; therefore, it is relevant and attractive.* We invited nonbelievers to accept the faith on the basis of its biblical, objective merits. *The Bible says* was all the authority our truth claims required.

In the postmodern culture we must use exactly the opposite strategy. That is, our faith must be attractive; then it can be relevant; then it might be true for its followers. *If we can show seekers of spiritual meaning that Christianity is attractive, interesting, and appealing, they will likely be willing to explore its relevance for their lives.* When they see its relevance and transforming effect in our lives, they may decide to try it for themselves. And when it "works," they will decide that it is true for them. They will affirm the authority of the Bible and its relevance for their lives, not in order to come to faith but because they have already come to faith.

Conclusion: Remembering Our Future

Can such an approach be effective? If we jettison our "truth first" approach to biblical authority and begin appealing to our culture on the basis of attractive relevance, will we abandon our Scriptural heritage? No. We will return to it.

We live in a postmodern, post-denominational, post-Christian culture. The first Christians lived in a pre-modern, pre-denominational, pre-Christian world. They had no hope of taking the gospel to the "ends of the earth" by appealing to the Roman Empire on the basis of biblical authority. The larger Greek world shared today's postmodern skepticism of any absolute truth claims, let alone those made on the basis of Hebrew Scriptures or a Jewish carpenter's teachings.

So the apostolic Christians built their evangelistic efforts on personal relevance and practical ministry. The result was the beginning of the most powerful, popular, and far-reaching religious movement in history.

I am convinced that we are now living in a culture more like that of the apostolic Christians than any we have seen since their day. They had no buildings or institutions to which they could invite a skeptical world. So they went *to* that world with the gospel. They had no objective authority base from which to work. So they demonstrated the authority of the Scriptures by their attractive, personal relevance.

We live in a day when nonbelievers will not come to our buildings to listen to our appeals on the basis of Scriptural authority. But when we show them the pragmatic value of biblical truth in our lives, ministries, and community, we will gain a hearing.

Postmodernity offers us a compelling opportunity to *remember our future*—to remember the biblical strategies on which the Christian movement was founded, and to rebuild our ministries on their foundation; to move into our postmodern future on the basis of our pre-modern heritage.

Our ministry strategies must therefore change from programs to people. Rather than staging religious events and waiting for the community to come to us, we will go to them on the basis of their needs. We will find issues and problems in the community that we can address. We will create need-centered ministries such as divorce recovery, survivors of suicide, single parenting, pre-marital classes, and coping with loss. Our members will look for ways to meet the personal needs of their neighbors, colleagues, and friends.

Once we have earned a hearing through our compassion and personal engagement in our hurting culture, we then share the reasons we care. We explain the difference that biblical truth has made in our lives. We prove that the Scriptures are true by their transforming personal effect. We live as people who pray for and believe in God's miraculous power. In such ways, many of the people we love and help will want what they see in us.

Our lives are the only Bibles many people will read today. So we show them God's love in ours. And those who reject "truth" but seek relevance will find what they are looking for in our faith. They will come to believe in biblical authority because they have experienced its effect personally. This was precisely how the first-century pagan world came to accept the truth of God's word. It is how we can promote the Scriptures in the twenty-first century as well.

People today are looking for a faith that is practical, loving, and hopeful. The tragedy is that our churches have not always offered them this biblical truth in a way that is attractive and relevant. The good news is that we can.

CHAPTER *Nine*

The Bible Is an Inspired Book

Biblical Authority and the Nature of God's Word

WHEN CLAUDE PEPPER WAS RUNNING for senator from Florida in 1950, one of his opponents attacked him this way: "Are you aware that Claude Pepper is known all over Washington as a shameless extrovert? He also practiced nepotism with his sister-in-law, and has a sister who was once a thespian in wicked New York City. Worst of all, before his marriage he habitually practiced celibacy!" Mr. Pepper lost the election.

Words matter. Words about the Bible matter, too.

As we continue our study of biblical authority, we come to these practical questions: What are we to call this book? What words best describe its authority? Which terms should we avoid, and which should we encourage? And why does it all matter?

Let's learn what the Bible says about itself, and then discuss some of the popular words for biblical authority in Baptist and church life today. Believe it or not, we'll not discuss a more volatile subject in this entire handbook.

God's Word on God's Word

We'll start our very brief tour within the pages of the Bible itself. Does this book consider itself to be authoritative? Or do those of us who affirm the timeless truth of Scripture misunderstand the book we defend? Critics of the sixteenth-century reformers accused them of making a "paper pope" of Scripture. Is our commitment to biblical authority warranted by the Bible itself? What does God's word say about itself?

What the Bible calls itself

The "Holy Bible" means *God's book*. The word *bible* comes from the ancient town of Byblos in Phoenicia, on the eastern edge of the Mediterranean Sea. Papyrus grown near Byblos and exported through its port was used to make the "paper" of the day.

A *bible*, then, is something written on *byblos* leaves or *papyrus*/paper. In other words, it is a book. While books called "the bible of home repair" or "the bible of computing" offend some of us, the word *bible* in these titles is actually being used in its most historical setting.

The name that distinguishes the Bible from all other books is "Holy." This word means to be divine or set apart. Think about it. The God who formed the universe also wrote a book. You have a copy of it.

This book sometimes is called the "Scriptures," a word that means God's "writings" (*script*) to us:

- Paul "vigorously refuted the Jews in public debate, proving from the Scriptures that Jesus was the Christ" (Acts 18:28).
- Paul reminded Timothy, "from infancy you have known the holy Scriptures, which are able to make you wise for salvation through faith in Christ Jesus. All Scripture is God-breathed and is useful for teaching, rebuking, correcting and training in righteousness, so that the man of God may be thoroughly equipped for every good work" (2 Timothy 3:15–16).

- Peter warned that "ignorant and unstable people" distort Paul's letters, "as they do other Scriptures, to their own destruction" (2 Peter 3:16).

The Bible also calls itself the "word of God":

- Jesus rebuked the religious authorities who "nullify the word of God for the sake of your tradition" (Matthew 15:6).
- Our Lord spoke of those "to whom the word of God came" (John 10:35).
- "The word of God is living and active. Sharper than any double-edged sword, it penetrates even to dividing soul and spirit, joints and marrow; it judges the thoughts and attitudes of the heart" (Hebrews 4:12).

The Bible doesn't just contain the words of God; it is the word of God.

The Bible on its origin

The Author of this book made the most stupendous claim in all of recorded literature: "All authority in heaven and on earth has been given to me" (Matt. 28:18). No Caesar, general, or dictator ever thought to claim all authority over the entire universe. If Jesus possesses "all" authority over every dimension of reality, how much authority do you and I have? The words given to us by such a Person obviously become the most significant and authoritative in all the world.

The Bible agrees. It claims to be *inspired* (*breathed into*) by its Author: "All Scripture is God-breathed" (2 Tim. 3:16). It claims divine, not human, authorship for its source: "Above all, you must understand that no prophecy of Scripture came about by the prophet's own interpretation. For prophecy never had its origin in the will of man, but men spoke from God as they were carried along by the Holy Spirit" (2 Pet. 1:20–21).

Paul says of his words, "The gospel I preached is not something that man made up. I did not receive it from any man, nor was I taught it; rather, I received it by revelation from Jesus Christ" (Galatians 1:11–12).

He made a similar statement to the Corinthians: "This is what we speak, not in words taught us by human wisdom but in words taught by the Spirit" (1 Corinthians 2:13).

Scripture claims to possess this divine authority for all time:

- "The grass withers and the flowers fall, but the word of our God stands forever" (Isaiah 40:8).
- After quoting this passage, Peter adds, "And this is the word that was preached to you" (1 Peter 1:25).
- Jesus was clear and adamant: "My words will never pass away" (Matthew 24:35).

The Bible claims to be the authoritative word of God on every subject it addresses. It asserts that its truths are objective and eternally relevant. It could not possibly claim a higher authority for itself.

Relating the divine and the human

So we know that the Bible is literally "God's word," given to humans through human agency. How did God use people to get his word to humankind? Here we must consider theories of inspiration of the Bible.

First, let's dispense with mistaken approaches. Some consider the Bible to be inspired like all great literature—no more. This is the *natural inspiration* theory. Others believe that the Bible was inspired to the same degree as Christian writing, preaching, and teaching today. This is the *general Christian* theory. Still others accept as inspired only certain sections of Scripture. This is the *partial inspiration* approach. The Bible rejects all three by claiming God's special authorship of all the Scriptures (2 Tim. 3:16).

Now let's consider the three most popular theories in Baptist and church life today. One is the *dictation* approach. By this view, God gave the literal words of Scripture directly to their human writers. The authors functioned something like stenographers. Some of the Bible clearly came to exist in this way (the Ten Commandments, for instance). But we find different vocabularies, writing styles, and goals within the various books. For this reason, the dictation theory is not popular with most scholars today.

The *verbal* approach suggests that God inspired the individual words of the Bible while also allowing human personality to be used. This view is usually combined with *plenary*, meaning *all*. It teaches that God took the initiative in inspiring each of the individual words of Scripture, but God did this in a way that engaged their personalities as well.

A third approach is the *dynamic* theory. Those who hold this view believe that God guided the writers more often than he gave each word to them. In this way their personalities were used, while God's purpose was achieved. This approach, while not insisting on the direct verbal inspiration of each word of the text, still maintains the divine inspiration of the Scriptures. This view affirms that inspiration is verbal not so much in its method as in its result.

Which approach is best? All three contain ideas that should be combined into one concept. We should affirm both the divine and the human elements behind the creation of Scripture, without allowing either to minimize the other.

Sometimes God dictated his words; sometimes God gave the authors his words in very direct ways (dreams and visions, for instance); and sometimes they used their own vocabularies to express the truth God gave them. Perhaps an analogy will help. Many writers, both ancient and modern, have compared the divine/human authorship of Scripture to the divine/human nature of its subject, Jesus Christ. Jesus was fully divine, but fully human as well. We cannot understand this mystery fully, but we can affirm it. In the same way, Scripture can be the very word of God, and yet use the words of human beings.

All significant spiritual truth requires the acceptance of paradox. God is three and yet one; the Lord is sovereign while we have free will. Jesus is fully God and fully human. God's word retains both the divine and the human as well.

Those closest to the text

The first Christians were convinced of the divine, authoritative nature of Scripture. They were clear on the fact that the Bible is the absolute, authoritative word of God. For instance, Peter cited Old Testament prophets as his authority in his Pentecost address, the first Christian sermon (Acts 2). Stephen's defense of the Christian faith was largely a retelling of Israel's history in the biblical narrative (Acts 7). James argued for Gentile inclusion in the church on the basis of biblical prophetic witness (Acts 15:16–18; Amos 9:11, 12).

Much of Paul's ministry was spent explaining how Jesus fulfilled Old Testament Messianic promises. An early example from his first missionary journey: "From Perga they went on to Pisidian Antioch. On the Sabbath they entered the synagogue and sat down. After reading from the Law and the Prophets, the synagogue rulers sent word to them, saying, 'Brothers, if you have a message of encouragement for the people, please speak'" (Acts 13:14–15). Paul immediately recited the biblical history of his people (Acts 13:16–22) and showed the people how Jesus fulfilled their Scriptures (Acts 13:23–31). He then claimed Psalm 2:7 (13:33), Isaiah 55:3 (13:34), Psalm 16:10 (13:35), and Habakkuk 1:5 (13:41) as warrant for the gospel he proclaimed.

The letters of the New Testament and early Christian history are filled with biblical citations. In fact, if we had only the letters written by second-century Christians we could reconstruct most of the New Testament on the basis of their voluminous quotations. There is no doubt that the first Christians considered the Bible to be the authoritative revelation and word of God. Critics can say they were right or they were wrong, but they cannot say they were ambiguous. These men and women would rather die than deny the truths they found in God's word.

The Bible and Inerrancy

The Bible calls itself the "inspired" word of God (see 2 Tim. 3:16, NASB, NRSV). As such, it is absolute, authoritative, and trustworthy. Baptists have affirmed these adjectives in describing Scripture all across our history (see chapter one).

In recent years, another term for biblical authority has been the subject of wide and heated debate: the *inerrancy* of Scripture. Some insist that we must use this word if we believe the Bible to be completely reliable and trustworthy. Others believe the word to be more political and confusing than theologically helpful. Which is right?

What does inerrancy mean?

Let's begin with some definitions. The word *inerrancy* has been used with regard to the Bible in divergent and contradictory ways across recent generations. So 300 or so scholars gathered in Chicago in 1978 to attempt a general definition of the term. The resulting statement, with nineteen articles of affirmation and denial, is called "The Chicago Statement on Biblical Inerrancy." It has been widely circulated and is the best-known statement on the subject today. Unfortunately, this noteworthy effort has not resolved the confusion that still surrounds the word.

Today at least eight different definitions of inerrancy are to be found in the works of leading conservative scholars. The list is by no means exhaustive, as still other approaches will undoubtedly be developed in the future. However, the list does illustrate the difficulty with using inerrancy as a simple test to determine whether someone believes the Bible.

Here are the most common definitions of the term *inerrancy*:

- A *general* definition: "Inerrancy simply means that the Bible can be trusted in what it teaches and affirms."[1] This statement by Clark Pinnock is probably the most popular approach to the word. However, it adds no clarification over what Baptists have always believed and said about Scripture.
- *Formal* inerrancy claims that "Scripture does not contradict itself."[2]
- *Material* inerrancy expands the above definition greatly: "Scripture does not lie or deceive in any assertion it makes."[3] The Chicago Statement offers a similar definition: "'Inerrancy signifies the quality of being free from all falsehood or mistake and so safeguards the truth that Holy Scripture is entirely true and trustworthy in all its assertions."[4]

- *Soteriological* inerrancy: the Bible is inerrant in all its teachings regarding salvation. The Roman Catholic Church adopted this position at Vatican II: "the books of Scripture must be acknowledged as teaching firmly, faithfully, and without error that truth which God wanted to put into the sacred writings for the sake of salvation."[5]
- *Limited* inerrancy claims that the Bible is without error in matters of faith and morals, but may or may not contain errors in other areas such as science, geography, and history.[6]
- *Indefectability* would state that the truth of Scripture is inerrant, but not necessarily its words.[7]
- *Secondary* inerrancy applies to the quotations and speeches recorded in Scripture, but does not guarantee that their content is free from error.[8] For instance, Luke records Stephen's speech in Acts 7 exactly as he gave it, although Stephen's words may not have been inerrant.
- *Purposive* or *intentional* inerrancy states that the Bible is inerrant in accomplishing its intended purpose, whatever that purpose might be. As Pinnock states, "inerrancy is relative to the intention of the text."[9] Advocates of this approach note that the Bible does not intend to be a book of science, history, or geography.

As you can see, these eight definitions vary significantly from one another. If someone asks you if you believe the Bible to be *inerrant*, ask the definition he or she means. Otherwise, your conversation may not clarify biblical authority at all.

How is the term qualified?

The problems with *inerrancy* as a term don't stop with its definitions. There are also many ways its users qualify the term. I'll list those employed by adherents of the *material inerrancy* view, the strongest approach to inerrancy:

- Inerrancy applies only to the original manuscripts, none of which we possess today.

- It does not imply verbal exactness of quotations. The New Testament writers may not quote the Old Testament or other sources with precise accuracy.
- It does not imply verbal or intentional agreement in parallel accounts of the same event.
- It does not preclude figurative speech, rounding of numbers, and other imprecisions of language.
- It does not preclude popular phrases and expressions such as "four corners of the earth."
- It does not require scientifically precise language in describing the things of nature.
- It does not preclude the use of mythology or folklore.
- It does not require historiography of modern standards. Chronology, genealogy, and other matters of historical record can be imprecise and interpretive.
- It does not require that the biblical author understood the full divine implications of his words (see Matt. 2:15 and Hosea 11:1).
- It does not preclude the use of non-precise descriptions of biblical books (see Proverbs 1:1, where the book is attributed to Solomon even though others wrote parts of the text; see Prov. 30–31).
- It does not require etymologies of words (origins of words) in the modern sense.
- It is to be accepted as a faith assertion, not the result of inductive study of the text at hand.[10]

These twelve qualifications must be added to the eight definitions, before we know what we mean by inerrancy. Such challenges make the word a difficult term to use in popular conversation, or even theological discourse.

The logic of inerrancy

As we noted above, the first qualification of inerrancy is that it applies only to the original manuscripts. We do not possess these.

The Chicago Statement admits that the copies we do possess are "not entirely error-free."[11]

Here's the problem. *If the Bible must be inerrant to be trustworthy, and if only the autographs are inerrant, by definition the copies we possess are errant and not trustworthy.* This conclusion is not the intention of those who promote *inerrancy*, but it is the logical result of their argument. Of course though, we *do* believe that the Bible we use is trustworthy.

Inerrancy and history

Harold Lindsell has argued strongly that inerrancy has been affirmed throughout Christian history.[12] However, Lindsell admits that the biblical writers "devoted little space to the careful formulation of a doctrine of revelation, inspiration, and inerrancy. Nowhere in Scripture is there any reasoned argument along this line."[13]

In church history, Origen is considered by Lindsell to be an inerrantist. But note Origen's allegorical method of interpretation, by which Jesus' colt in the Triumphal Entry is the Old Testament, carrying him to the cross.[14] Augustine is likewise considered an inerrantist; but remember his allegorical interpretation of the Parable of the Good Samaritan, where the oil and wine are baptism and the inn is the church.[15] Clearly, inerrancy does not protect us from theological error.

The doctrine of inerrancy was formulated formally by Francis Turretin, a seventeenth-century theologian. With Turretin we see the first form of the inerrancy argument in church history. His work highly influenced Princeton Seminary. His *Institutio Theologiae Elencticae* became the principal textbook in systematic theology at Princeton from 1812 until 1872.[16]

What of inerrancy in Baptist history? Historian Mark Noll characterizes the Baptist doctrine of authority as functional—we know the Bible is true because it works in our lives.[17] Baptist confessions of faith were happy to characterize Scripture as "truth without mixture of error" (see chapter one). But Baptists did not formulate a specific doctrine of inerrancy until this generation.

Bible passages and inerrancy

Supporters of inerrancy point quickly to Bible passages that they believe require the use of the word. Let's consider them briefly, with the supposed synonym for inerrancy or key word in italics in the Bible quotation.

- Numbers 23:19: "God is not a man, that he should *lie*, nor a son of man, that he should change his mind." The suggestion is that since the Bible is inspired by God, it cannot "lie" and therefore must be inerrant. But "lie" and *error* are not the same thing. Too, the text in question intends to speak not to the Bible but to the character of God himself.
- Psalm 12:6: "And the words of the Lord are *flawless*." The Hebrew root is *taher*, which refers to ritual or moral purity, particularly to a person as being clean enough to return to life within the nation of Israel. The Bible would never call such a person *inerrant*.[18] The reference is to being clean and pure.
- Psalm 18:30: "As for God, his way is perfect; the word of the Lord is *flawless*." Here we find a different Hebrew word, *sarap*. The word refers to metal that is refined, and it could never imply that such material is inerrant or perfect.[19]
- Psalm 19:7: "The law of the Lord is *perfect*, reviving the soul. The statutes of the Lord are *trustworthy*, making wise the simple." "Perfect" translates *tamam*, which means to be *complete*, something that accomplishes its purpose.[20] "Trustworthy" is from *aman*, which means *to be firm, certain, or faithful* to the task.[21] Neither word implies inerrancy.
- Psalm 119:142: "Your righteousness is everlasting and your law is *true*." "True" translates *emet*, a derivative of *aman*, discussed with reference to Psalm 19:7 above.
- John 10:35: " . . . The Scripture cannot be *broken*." "Broken" translates *luthanai*, from *luo*. It means *to nullify*[22] and has no reference to inerrancy.
- John 17:17: "Sanctify them by the truth; your word is *truth*." Truth translates *alatheia*. Greek scholar A. T. Robertson

suggests the meaning here to be "God's message" as opposed to "human speculation."[23]

- Romans 7:12: "So, then, the law is *holy*, and the commandment is holy, righteous, and good." "Holy" translates *hagios,* which means to be dedicated to God. Scripture is "holy" because it belongs to God; inerrancy is not in view here.
- 2 Timothy 3:15: ". . . and how from infancy you have known the *holy* Scriptures." "Holy" translates *hieros,* which means to be consecrated to God.[24]

In each case, the word in question has no intended connection to the argument for inerrancy.

The origins of inerrancy

If the inerrant approach to Scripture does not come from Scripture, where does it originate? The answer is found with Aristotle (384–322 B.C.), the first philosopher to formalize the laws of logic we use today. His foundational concept was the *law of contradiction.* Either *A* is *B* or *A* is not *B*; it cannot be both. The sun will rise tomorrow or the sun will not rise tomorrow; both statements cannot be true.

The *law of contradiction* is extremely useful in such fields as medicine and biology, Aristotle's intended applications. But taken to theology, it causes difficulty. Is God three or one? Was Jesus fully divine or fully human? Does God know the future or do we have freedom of choice? In each case, the answer is *yes.*

Inerrancy is a logical, Aristotelian argument that theologians have applied to the Bible; it is not an argument found within Scripture itself. Is the Bible inerrant or errant? That is a question asked by Greek logic, not by the biblical text.

As a result, whenever inerrantists try to use Scripture to support their position, they must always employ a logical progression to do so. *God inspired the Bible, God doesn't err, and so the Bible doesn't err* is an argument from logic, not Scripture. There's not a single biblical text that reasons in this way.

When we ask questions the Bible does not intend to answer, we get in trouble every time. If we ask the Scriptures for an involved scientific explanation of the origin of the universe, we'll be disappointed. This is simply not the purpose of Genesis. If we seek a detailed system for the future from God's word, we'll be frustrated. A basic principle for all study of literature is to find and follow the author's intended purpose. Nowhere is this more important than in studying the Bible.

Conclusion

So what's the best way to describe biblical authority? The best way is the way the Bible describes itself: as the "inspired" word of God. As God's inspired word, the Bible helps us understand the meaning of what God has done. The Bible is the witness of all that God has done to redeem his people and reconcile the world to himself. We can rely on it completely.

I believe in and preach wholeheartedly the absolute trustworthiness of God's word. The Bible—can we believe it? Yes!

CHAPTER Ten
The Bible Is a Practical Book

Biblical Authority and the Study of God's Word: Part One

WHEN I WAS A COLLEGE student, I served as a Baptist Student Union missionary in East Malaysia, on the island of Borneo in Southeast Asia. Missionaries in Singapore had given my partner and me a duffel bag filled with paperback Malay New Testaments. At our first church, we passed them out. The people stood in line for over an hour in the hot sun, waiting to receive a copy of God's word in their language. Most of them had never before owned a Bible.

I'll never forget the elderly woman who stood at the end of the line. Patiently she waited. Finally it was her turn. I handed her a paperback New Testament. Her hands trembled as she held it close to her heart, tears running down her face. I thought of all my Bibles at home gathering dust. I didn't have to wonder whether she would read what she had received.

Biblical authority is of little practical good in our lives unless it leads to biblical study. We may believe that Scripture is divinely inspired, that it stands up to every test and critique from a skeptical world. But if we do not put its truths into practice in our lives, our beliefs don't affect our lives. The purpose of God's word is to change those who read it, molding us in the image of Jesus (Romans 8:29).

So, how can you meet God in his word? How can you study the Bible for yourself? In this chapter we'll look at preparations necessary for effective Bible study. In the next chapter we'll discover guidelines that apply to every passage in Scripture and explore principles that relate to specific sections of God's word.

Personal Preparations

We will begin to focus now on what is known as "general hermeneutics."[1] Hermes was the messenger god; "hermeneutics" is therefore the study of a message or principles of interpretation. Biblical hermeneutics is the field of study that identifies necessary rules and guidelines for Bible study.

Before we can use such principles, however, we must first make three personal commitments. Because the Bible is God's word, not the product of human knowledge and study, we must be ready spiritually to hear what it says to us.

Meet God personally

First, you must know the Author of this book personally. Paul warned the Corinthians, "The man without the Spirit does not accept the things that come from the Spirit of God, for they are foolishness to him, and he cannot understand them, because they are spiritually discerned" (1 Corinthians 2:14).

Paul does not mean that an unconverted person can understand nothing in the Bible. Rather, Paul teaches that we cannot "accept" or "understand" the spiritual applications of Scripture unless the Holy Spirit guides us to such interpretation. God's word will remain on the level of fact and knowledge, without penetrating to our hearts and changing us. We must have a personal relationship with Jesus before God's word can accomplish its intended purpose in our lives.

For many years I thought I was a Christian, since I believed in God and tried to be a good person. Most Americans think my definition of Christianity is correct. We are self-made people who believe in morality and religion. As long as a person believes God exists and tries to live by "the good book," we think we don't really need to know what "the good book" says. I never went to church or studied Scripture, but I thought I would go to heaven when I died.

When I was fifteen, a Baptist church in our part of Houston, Texas, started a bus ministry. They bought an old school bus, painted the church's name on the side, and started looking for people who would ride it to church. In August of 1973 some people from the church knocked on the door of our apartment. My younger brother and I didn't want to go to church, but our father put us on the bus. I heard the gospel for the first time.

As I came to church and Sunday School, I began to sense that these people had a joy and purpose I had never discovered. So a few weeks later, I asked my Sunday School teacher how I could have what the others in the class had. She led me to personal faith in Christ that day. Six months later, my brother came to faith. A year later, we were baptized together. He is now pastor of First Baptist Church in Gainesville, Texas.

I was attracted to Christ by Christians. People who studied Scripture and applied its truths to their lives were different from me. I wanted what I saw in them. But I couldn't understand the truths by which they lived until I made their Lord mine.

We cannot understand the Bible unless we know first its Author. Have you met him?

Be willing to work hard

Paul challenged his young apprentice in the ministry, "Devote yourself to the public reading of Scripture, to preaching and to teaching" (1 Timothy 4:13). "Devote yourself" translates a Greek term that requires previous, private preparations.[2] Like any area of intellectual investigation, understanding and applying the Scriptures requires personal work. The more you invest, the greater the return.

Ministry students sometimes tell me they want to pastor a "New Testament church." I always ask them which one. I'd enjoy pastoring in Antioch, not so much in Corinth. According to Paul, one of the Corinthian problems was their immaturity: "Brothers, I could not address you as spiritual but as worldly—mere infants in Christ. I gave you milk, not solid food, for you were not yet ready for it. Indeed, you are still not ready. You are still worldly" (1 Corinthians 3:1–3). Milk is food digested by a mother and made palatable for her child. Unfortunately, the Corinthians wanted their spiritual truth the same way—digested by someone else.

Many Christians suffer from the Corinthian desire to let others study Scripture for them. *That's what we pay a pastor for*, they say. *I've not been to seminary; I don't have time to study the Bible; so I'll listen to my minister or Sunday school teacher. I'll let the professionals do it.* But as we learned in chapter two, the Bible is meant for every believer. Baptists affirm strongly the priesthood of every Christian. You are privileged and responsible to interpret God's word for yourself.

In this chapter we'll learn how to use the various tools of Bible study. Translations, commentaries, and a Bible dictionary, concordance, atlas, and encyclopedia will all help. But these tools are meant to assist your study, not replace it. Christianity is not a spectator sport. Decide you are willing to work hard to meet God in God's word.

Obey what you discover

The Bible is not meant to inform our minds as much as it intends to change our lives. Jesus said, "If any one chooses to do God's will, he will find out whether my teaching comes from God or whether I speak on my own" (John 7:17). Obedience leads to relationship. Faith is required. We must position ourselves to receive what God wants to give by grace. The Israelites had to step into the flooded Jordan River before God would stop its flow (Joshua 3:15–16).

Decide before you open God's word that you will obey what you find there. Write your Father a blank check of obedience. God will not reveal his will as an option to consider, but as an order to follow. If you will not do what God says, you'll not understand what God says. No father can lead a child who is unwilling to follow.

Guiding Presuppositions

My high school geometry class acquainted me with the concept of axioms. These are unprovable presuppositions, guiding beliefs that are basic to the study of mathematics. We cannot prove that parallel lines never intersect, but we accept this principle in the study of geometry. All knowledge is built on such presuppositions. Scientists believe the physical universe to be stable and predictable. Otherwise, experiments could never be repeated.

Bible study is built on certain presuppositions as well. Three are especially important to our interpretation of God's word.

Believe that you can understand Scripture

Luther and the Reformers were adamant: the Bible can be understood. God has given us his revelation in such a way that we can discover and apply its truths. We need not depend on creeds, councils, and church tradition. Every believer is his or her own priest before God and God's word.

So we will begin Bible study with the Bible—not with the teachings of the church on a particular subject, but with the teachings of Scripture. We will ask theologians and church teachings to guide us along the way, believing that we can learn from others as we study. Indeed, we can learn much as we study the Bible with our fellow Christians and test our individual interpretations and understanding with them. But we will not allow the opinions of humans to replace the revelation of God.

Use the New Testament to interpret the Old

As we learned in chapter one, Baptists believe that "the criterion by which the Bible is to be interpreted is Jesus Christ."[3] We agree with John that Scripture exists to lead us to faith in Jesus (John 20:30–31). The New Testament, which reveals Christ, is therefore our means of interpreting the Old Testament, which prepares the way for Christ. As Christ said repeatedly, he fulfills the Scriptures that told the world of his coming (see Matthew 5:17).

In other words, we will study Scripture according to the theological doctrine of *progressive revelation*. We believe that God reveals himself progressively, building later revelation on earlier truth. As a mathematics teacher must teach arithmetic before she can teach geometry, and trigonometry before she can discuss calculus, so God reveals himself progressively to us. Upon the foundation of the Old Testament law, God spoke through his prophets. They in turn focused on the Messiah, God's personal revelation. The New Testament builds on this revelation in a Person through revelation in words. The New Testament is therefore our means of interpreting his earlier revelation.

This guiding presupposition leads to an important principle, one we will meet again in the next chapter. Whenever an Old Testament law is renewed in the New Testament, it retains the force of law for Christians today. For instance, by endorsing the Ten Commandments, Jesus made them obligatory for his followers (Matthew 19:16–19).

On the other hand, any Old Testament law not renewed in the New Testament retains the force of principle for Christian living. For instance, the Jewish dietary codes were made non-binding on Gentile converts by the Jerusalem Council (Acts 15:28–29; see also 10:9—11:18; Galatians 2:11–14). However, these laws still demonstrate the relevant principle that God cares about our physical health. We will study them to discover principles and truths that apply to our lives as we relate to God through grace.

Make the Bible its own commentary

Our third guiding presupposition is that the Scriptures interpret themselves. Because God's word is unified, coherent, and fully inspired, every word is the word of God. So the best way to study any single passage is to interpret it in light of the rest of the Bible. We will seek to compare Scripture with Scripture, interpreting the part by the whole.

Five important principles emerge from this presupposition.

First, interpret unclear passages in light of clear truth. Study the difficult parts of Scripture in light of its clear teachings. For instance, Jesus told his disciples, "If anyone comes to me and does not hate his father and mother, his wife and children, his brothers and sisters—yes, even his own life—he cannot be my disciple" (Luke 14:26).

Does Jesus condemn the family? Absolutely not. Matthew's Gospel explains: "Anyone who loves his father or mother more than me is not worthy of me; anyone who loves his son or daughter more than me is not worthy of me" (Matt.10:37). Luke's version means that we are to "hate" our families in the sense that we place them under Jesus in priority and commitment. The clear version helps us understand the more difficult.

Additionally, the New Testament contains other clear teachings that affirm the value of the family (see 1 Corinthians 9:5; 1 Timothy 5:8; Ephesians 5:25). These clear references help us understand and apply Jesus' teachings to our lives.

Second, do not base doctrine on only one text. Consider the "millennium," found explicitly only in Revelation 20:1–6. This is obviously an important subject, but it should not be made a test of orthodoxy. At least seven theories on the subject are held by Bible-believing scholars. No person's belief in biblical authority should be questioned because of his or her theory on the millennium. We should seek to build major doctrines on more extensive biblical texts.

Another example is Paul's question of the Corinthians, "if there is no resurrection, what will those do who are baptized for the dead?" (1 Cor. 15:29). This is not the place to discuss various ways of interpreting this passage. Just know that the Bible makes no other reference to being "baptized for the dead." Do not build a larger doctrine on this single verse.

Third, study brief passages in light of longer texts. Interpret a single verse in light of the larger passage in which it is found, that passage in light of its book, and the book in light of the entire Bible. As you consider the larger counsel of God's word, you will allow Scripture to interpret itself.

Fourth, apply doctrine taught in various parts of Scripture to all times and cultures. A variety of contexts and circumstances lie behind the various passages of God's word. Whenever a statement is found in a number of different contexts and is taught by a variety of biblical authors, we may know that it was intended as a timeless statement of truth. If it is taught only by one author in one place, we can know that it was a specific statement for that time and context. It will apply in principle to our lives, but perhaps not as a command. In this sense, it is like an Old Testament law not renewed in the New; it teaches spiritual truth but not binding obligation.

One controversial example of this principle regards the biblical teachings on the subject of homosexuality. It is claimed by some who defend this lifestyle that the scriptural prohibitions are culturally conditioned, that they apply only to that time and place.

Those who interpret Scripture this way would do well to follow the principle under discussion here. The Bible comments on homosexuality seven times, across both the Old and New Testaments, in a variety of cultural contexts:

- In Genesis 19 we find the attempt by men in Sodom to "have sex" with Lot's angelic visitors (19:5), and we find also God's consequent punishment against the city. While homosexual practice is clearly part of the text, the passage is less clear as to whether God's judgment was against homosexuality itself, or the crowd's abusive attempt to commit homosexual rape.
- Leviticus 18:22 and Leviticus 20:13 clearly prohibit homosexual activity.
- Deuteronomy 23:17–18 outlaws all prostitution, whether male or female.
- Romans 1:26–27 describes homosexual acts as "unnatural" and "indecent."
- 1 Corinthians 6:9–10 and 1 Timothy 1:8–11 are considered by some to refer to homosexual prostitution. However, these texts seem more objectively to forbid homosexual practice in any context.

Additionally, no biblical passage can be cited with confidence as an endorsement of this activity. No biblical leader or ethical model taught by the Scriptures can be construed accurately as practicing this lifestyle.

Here's the point for our discussion: when the Bible speaks across cultures and contexts to a subject, we can take its words to be equally relevant to all time and circumstances.

Fifth, if two biblical statements appear humanly to contradict, accept both. Divine truth is not bound by human logic, and often must be expressed by two statements that appear to contradict each other. This is known as *antinomy*, meaning *the acceptance of two principles that seem mutually exclusive but are each independently true.*

For example, I am often asked about freedom and divine sovereignty. If we have complete freedom of will, is God's knowledge and control of the future limited? Or, if God knows the future, how can we have freedom to choose?

In truth, the Bible often states both principles. Jesus stated both principles in the same sentence: "The Son of Man will go as it has been decreed, but woe to that man who betrays him" (Luke 22:22).

In summary, these presuppositional decisions will guide you in interpreting and applying God's word accurately:

- Believe that you can understand Scripture yourself.
- Use the New Testament to interpret the Old Testament.
- Make the Bible its own commentary. As a result:
  (1) Interpret unclear passages in the light of clear truth.
  (2) Do not base doctrine on only one text.
  (3) Study brief passages in light of longer texts.
  (4) Apply doctrine taught in various parts of Scripture to all times and cultures.
  (5) If two biblical statements appear humanly to contradict, accept both.

Background Questions

Now we're ready to begin asking questions of the specific text we wish to study. As with any literature, we need to know certain facts before we can understand the author's intended meaning.

Who was the writer?

First, who wrote the text you will study? What can you learn about the writer's background, circumstances, and experiences? What was happening at the time the writer wrote the book you're about to read?

Surely you've shared the frustrating experience of listening to only one side of a telephone conversation. You can understand every word being spoken at your end. But if you don't know the identity of the other person in the conversation, you can easily misinterpret what is being said.

Knowing the author and the author's circumstances bring much light to bear on the text at hand. For instance, many believers appreciate the Book of Philippians as a treatise on joy. Paul exhorts us, "Rejoice in the Lord always" (Philippians 4:4). His joy in writing to his Philippian friends is tangible and encouraging.

But when we learn Paul's circumstances at the time he wrote the letter, its theme becomes even more significant. Philippi was the first town to imprison Paul during his ministry. In fact, he and Silas were beaten severely before being locked into their jail cell (Acts 16:16–24). Now the apostle was in another jail cell, this one in Rome. He had no way of knowing if he would be released or face execution. Writing from a jail cell to the town where he was first in a jail cell, Paul could nonetheless celebrate his joy in Jesus.

"Joy in a jail cell" is a fitting title for the letter. Knowing the author and his circumstances makes the epistle even more transforming for us.

Who were the recipients?

The second question follows the first: To whom was the author writing? Were the first readers believers or unbelievers? persecuted or safe? a church, a group of churches, or an individual? What can you know about their circumstances, needs, and issues?

Why does Matthew quote the Old Testament more often than any other New Testament writer? Because the background of his audience was Jewish, and he wished to show them that Jesus was their Messiah. Why did Mark go to such lengths to explain Jewish customs (Mark 7:2–4; 15:42) and translate Aramaic words (3:17; 5:41; etc.)? Because he was writing to Gentiles, most probably in Rome.

Why did Luke employ more medical terminology in his Gospel and Acts than we find anywhere else in Scripture? Because he was a physician (Colossians 4:14). Why did John begin his first letter with the claim, "That which was from the beginning, which we have heard, which we have seen with our eyes, which we have looked at and our hands have touched—this we proclaim concerning the Word of life" (1 John 1:1)? Because every word you just read refutes incipient Gnosticism, a Greek philosophy that separated physical from spiritual and contended that Jesus could not be both divine and human. And this was John's purpose.

When you know the recipients of a biblical book, you will be able to join them. When you sit with the Philippians as they listen to Paul's letter, you'll be able to understand better its relevance for your life and needs today.

What was the author's purpose?

Writing in the ancient world was too hard to do without a compelling purpose. Today we drop a note in the mail or send an e-mail in a moment. Ancient writers paid a high price to produce the biblical books we read today.

As a result, we need to know all we can about the author's intended purpose before we try to interpret his writing. Much of Scripture was produced to accomplish a specific task or purpose. If we don't understand the task at hand, we'll miss much of what the writer wants us to know and do.

Often the text will make its purpose clear. John disclosed the express purpose of his Gospel: "Jesus did many other miraculous signs in the presence of his disciples, which are not recorded in this book. But these are written that you may believe that Jesus is the Christ, the Son of God, and that by believing you may have life in his name" (John 20:30–31).

John wanted to lead his readers to trust Jesus as their Messiah, so that they might find "life in his name." We would expect to find numerous signs and evidences of Jesus' divinity, and examples of the transforming power of his love. That's exactly what John gives us.

Note that Luke stated his explicit purpose at the beginning of his book (Luke 1:1-4), but John waited to the end to disclose his. When you are preparing to study a passage in Scripture, it is always a good idea to look over the larger book in which it is found. Find those statements that convey the purpose of the book, and interpret the specific text in light of that intention. Commentaries and encyclopedia articles can help in discovering the purpose of the book. Be sure you have it in mind before proceeding in your Bible study.

What kind of literature is this?

Scripture contains a wide variety of literary styles within its pages. Unlike most books ancient and modern, the Bible is composed of many different kinds of literature, including history, law, poetry, letters, figures of speech, and apocalyptic literature. The way you interpret poetry is not the way you read the newspaper. When Robert Frost claims that "Two roads diverged in a yellow wood,"[4] we don't stop and ask for the location on a map.

Let's look briefly at the literary categories we find within Scripture.

History is the literature of Genesis, Exodus 1—19, Numbers to Esther, portions of the prophets, Gospels, and Acts. It should be read as factual narrative, seeking truths and principles within the events themselves. We should avoid seeking symbolic or spiritual meaning within historical occurrences. Easter is a fact of history, not merely the resurrection of faith in Jesus' disciples.

Law is found primarily in Exodus 20—40 and Leviticus. It should be read to discover principles for living today, except where it is renewed in the New Testament and continues as law for Christian faith and practice.

Poetry is used from Job to the Song of Solomon, and in other places throughout Scripture. It should be read symbolically, without pressing the details for historical accuracy or specific promises. For example, the psalmist promised, "The Lord watches over you—the Lord is your shade at your right hand; the sun will not harm you by day, nor the moon by night" (Psalm 121:5-6). This poetry deals with God's care for his own, and is obviously not concerned with sunburn or exposure. Interpret poetry in terms of its intended symbols and spiritual meaning.

Letters are found in the Old Testament prophets (see Jeremiah 29), and in the New Testament from Romans to Jude and in Revelation 2—3. They should always be read with their immediate audience and concerns in mind. We must not apply a letter's intended meaning to our situation until we are sure of the author's intended application to his audience.

Apocalyptic literature is found in Zechariah; Ezekiel; Daniel; Matthew 24—25; Mark 13; and Revelation. This material is highly visionary and tends to be symbolic and future-oriented. The method you choose for interpreting these books will largely determine the meanings you find there.

It is vital that we approach the book we are studying in a way that is consistent with its type of literature. Only then can we discover the intended meaning of the text, which is the object of all Bible study.

Conclusion

You may be surprised at how much this preliminary work will help you interpret the passage in question. Here you lay the foundation for all effective Bible study.

The preparations suggested by this chapter are vital to understanding any kind of literature, especially writings more than twenty centuries old. It is part of the miracle of God's word that when we make the investment of such preparations, the Scriptures come to life for us as if we were their intended audience. That's because in a very real way, we are.

CHAPTER Eleven

The Bible Is a Relevant Book

Biblical Authority and the Study of God's Word: Part Two

I'M LOOKING AT MY FIRST Bible as it sits on the credenza in my study. It is a red New Testament distributed by the Gideons at James Butler Bonham Elementary in Houston, Texas, on March 27, 1969. I know because I wrote that information in its flyleaf. When I received it, I began carrying it in the hip pocket of my jeans, accounting for its tattered condition today.

While I was pleased to have my own Bible, I couldn't do much with it. Like most first-time Bible students, I opened to the first page. There I found the *begats*. After three or four, I gave up. Clearly I didn't know enough to understand this book, I thought.

I was both right and wrong. As we discovered in the chapter ten, some preparations are necessary for studying any literature and especially God's word. As we will see in this chapter, there are principles and practices that guide all effective Bible study. These tools are intended for every person who wants to meet God in God's word.

As we begin our study of a specific passage, first we will ask the background questions of chapter ten. With this information in mind, we are ready to proceed.[1]

I will suggest in this chapter this fourfold approach to all Bible study:

- Grammatical: What do the words mean?
- Historical: What are the circumstances behind the text?
- Theological: What spiritual and theological truth does the text intend to communicate?
- Practical: What applications does the text intend to make in my life?

Grammatical Principles

We'll start with grammatical questions. Baptists believe that the Bible is intended for all believers, and that each believer is his or her own priest before God. So we come to the text in the belief that the intention is that we understand it.

Word study

Begin with the words themselves. We want to know what the author intended them to say, not just what they seem to say to us today. Words that survive long in any language acquire added meanings and implications. We want to know the meaning the author intended.

For instance, Jesus told us of a man who entrusted his servants with "talents" (Matthew 25:14–30). Today the word refers to gifts or abilities. In Jesus' day it was a measure of money (worth more than a thousand dollars in our currency). We misinterpret the parable if we think it relates to our God-given abilities and spiritual gifts.

The King James Version tells us that Zacchaeus wanted to see Jesus "and could not for the press, because he was little of stature" (Luke 19:3). We may picture this short man trying to see around the reporters who were interviewing Jesus on his way into Jericho. Of course, "press" in the seventeenth century meant *crowd*. Luke was not condemning the media.

How do we do a word study? Ask these five questions:

First, how was the word defined? With the help of a Bible dictionary, look up all unclear words in the passage. Be careful to confine your work to the definition of the word as it was intended by its original author.

Second, what is the context of the word? Often the sentences surrounding the term will explain its meaning. For example, Jesus referred to the kingdom of God in the Model Prayer (Matthew 6:10). What was this "kingdom"? Our Lord defined it himself: "your kingdom come, your will be done on earth as it is in heaven." Jesus used parallelism, a kind of Hebrew expression in which the second line repeats or defines the first. The "kingdom" is where God's will is done. The context defines the term.

Third, what is the history of the word? A dictionary or encyclopedia will provide its background and root meanings. But again, be careful to confine your interpretation to the intended meaning of the author. Too, use commentaries to help you work with the word in its original language.

Note that the history of the translated word may have little to do with the author's intended meaning. Consider "blessed," the word with which Jesus begins each of his Beatitudes (Matt. 5:3–11). The English word may come from the Old English word *bliss*, meaning *joy*. It could come from *blod*, referencing *blood sacrifice*. So someone is "blessed" if they have been atoned for by sacrifice. It may come from *benedicere*, a Latin word meaning *to wish well*. When I first preached on the Beatitudes as a college student, I used each of these definitions in my explanation of the word.

Only later did I realize that Jesus did not use our English word "blessed," but the Greek word *makarios*. And it has none of this background in its history. *Makarios* describes a happiness that transcends circumstances, a joy beyond words or the world. By importing definitions from the English translation, I missed the meaning of the original word. Don't do that.

Fourth, what are other biblical uses of the word? A concordance or dictionary will help here. Since Scripture interprets Scripture, other passages can often help clarify the meaning of the words of the text.

For instance, remember that Jesus warns us that one who calls someone a "fool" is in danger of the "fire of hell" (Matt. 5:22). Why? Because "fool" in the Bible describes a person of the worst moral deficiency, someone who rejects God for a life of terrible corruption. This is the person who "says in his heart, 'There is no God'" (Psalm 14:1). To call someone a "fool" was to malign the person's character and value, the worst form of insult.

Fifth, what is the cultural background behind the word? What practices current in the author's day affected his use of the term? Jesus told us, "If someone forces you to go one mile, go with him two" (Matt. 5:41). Was he talking about joggers out for a run, or bikers on a trail?

Actually, he referred to a Persian custom taken over by the Romans, by which a subject could be forced to carry a soldier's pack for one mile. This was done not to help the soldier as much as to remind the subject that he served the Empire. Jesus is saying, *If someone humiliates you, allow him to humiliate you even further. Don't return slander for slander, insult for insult. Treat even your enemies with humble service.* The cultural background clarifies the intention of the phrase.[2]

To summarize, begin your study of the biblical text with the words. Define and clarify their meaning, with the help of a dictionary, concordance, encyclopedia, and/or commentary. We must know the meaning of the words of God if we would interpret the word of God.

Sentence structure

Often the grammar of the Hebrew, Aramaic, or Greek text will affect its translated meaning for us. Here the sentence structure employed by the author is vital. A good commentary will help in this regard.

For an example of the importance of Hebrew sentence structure, consider Genesis 3:12: "The man said, 'The woman you put here with me—she gave me some of the fruit from the tree, and I ate it.'" Who was Adam blaming for his sin—the woman or the One who made her? The grammar answers the question.

The Hebrew words translate literally, "the woman / the man / and he said / with me / you gave / whom / the tree from / to me she gave / she / and I / ate." The use of "she" in the Hebrew subjective case before the verb places focus on the one performing the action. Adam was directly and emphatically blaming Eve for his sin. You don't need to know Hebrew to understand such a point. But you should consult a commentary written by someone who does.

An example of the significance of sentence structure in the Greek New Testament is 1 John 3:9. The King James Version translates the verse, "Whosoever is born of God doth not commit sin; for his seed remaineth in him: and he cannot sin, because he is born of God." This rendering has caused many people to question their salvation when they sin. If we are "born of God," we "cannot sin." Or so the text seems to say.

Here's good news for all of us who are God's children but still disappoint our Father. The Greek verbs refer to continued action. Thus the NIV translates, "No one who is born of God will continue to sin, because God's seed remains in him; he cannot go on sinning, because he has been born of God." The syntax makes the intended meaning clear.

Literary type

We discussed in chapter ten the importance of knowing the kind of literature used in the book we're studying. However, the specific text must also be considered in the same way. For instance, Matthew's Gospel contains symbols, teaching discourses, and apocalyptic sections. We will interpret a parable differently than we will an historical narrative.

Figures of speech are an important topic within the subject of literary type. One is the metaphor, an illustration using a direct comparison that is not intended to be understood literally. For instance, when Jesus called himself the "true vine" (John 15:1), he was clearly using metaphor.

Another figure of speech is the simile, a comparison that employs *like* or *as*. For example, "the sight of the glory of the Lord was like devouring fire" (Exodus 24:17, KJV) is a simile. A third figure is the hyperbole, a statement that uses exaggeration to make a point. Like the metaphor and simile, it is not intended to be interpreted literally.

When we read Jesus' admonition, "If your right eye causes you to sin, gouge it out and throw it away" (Matt. 5:29), it is vital that we interpret the text as Jesus intends!

Context

As we consider the grammatical dimensions of the passage we're studying, we want to study the larger context of the text. Ask three questions:

(1) What is the general idea of the larger passage where the text is found?
(2) How does the text contribute to the flow of the author's thought and intention?
(3) Is this passage teaching *prescriptive* or *descriptive* truth? This is a crucial issue in biblical hermeneutics.

Prescriptive statements are intended as commands for the reader. When Jesus warns us, "Do not judge, or you too will be judged" (Matt. 7:1), he prescribed behavior for all believers. On the other hand, descriptive statements simply disclose the event, without endorsing it as proper behavior. First Kings 11:3 states that Solomon had 700 wives and 300 concubines. The description does not prescribe such behavior for us.

Many of the wrong ideas that have been blamed on Scripture have originated in this area. Polygamists claim, *The Bible says Solomon had 700 wives, and so why can't we have several?* The Bible also says that the crowd wanted Jesus to be crucified, that Ananias and Sapphira tried to cheat the church, and that the town of Lystra stoned Paul and left him for dead. None of this behavior is prescribed for us today. Much of what we find in Scripture is there to warn us of what not to do.

As you study the text itself, think in contextual circles. Move from the text in question, to its chapter, to its section in the biblical book, to the book, to the Testament, to the rest of Scripture. As you understand the words in their intended meaning, you will make the most important single step to effective Bible study.

Historical Principles

The second major part of our fourfold approach concerns the historical background and context of the text. You will have already learned some of the history behind the text when you studied the individual words and their circumstances. Now you'll ask questions about the larger context and culture in which the text is found.

Geography

Locate the biblical event in its proper geographic circumstances. The more you know about the land where the event took place, the more you'll understand its text. It's a good investment of time to familiarize yourself with the basic layout of the Bible lands. You need a good atlas, or use the maps at the back of your Bible.

In addition, you'll need to know the geography behind any specific text you are studying. Two examples are often cited by hermeneutics textbooks in this regard.

First, consider Jeremiah 13:1–5:

> *This is what the Lord said to me: "Go and buy a linen belt and put it around your waist, but do not let it touch water." So I bought a belt, as the Lord directed, and put it around my waist. Then the word of the Lord came to me a second time: "Take the belt you bought and are wearing around your waist, and go now to Perath and hide it there in a crevice in the rocks." So I went and hid it at Perath, as the Lord told me.*

This seems a rather routine narrative, until we discover that Perath lay more than 400 miles from where Jeremiah received this command. The long, arduous trip described points up the sacrifice often necessary to obedience. The setting and intention of the text would not be clear unless we understood the geography as well as those who first read the passage.

A second example of geographic interpretation is found in Luke 2:4: "Joseph also went up from the town of Nazareth in Galilee to Judea, to Bethlehem the town of David." This was a journey of some ninety miles, made on a donkey's back by a woman who "was expecting a child" (Luke 2:5). Fulfilling God's promise that the Messiah would be born in Bethlehem (Micah 5:2) required great sacrifice for his mother. The geography of the text makes it alive and relevant.

In addition, Judea was "up" in elevation from Galilee, explaining the reference in the text. We typically think of "up" as north and are puzzled to learn that Joseph and Mary went "up" but south. The geographic context explains the text.

Social context

Knowing the customs or general historical situation often illuminates the biblical text. First, consider *material objects.* In Matthew 27:34 we read, "There [on the cross] they offered Jesus wine to drink, mixed with gall; but after tasting it, he refused to drink it." However, John 19:28–30 describes Jesus' requesting and drinking wine on the cross. Do the accounts contradict each other?

Not at all. The drink to which Matthew refers was a kind of narcotic often given to crucifixion victims to dull their senses. Jesus refused this anesthetic, choosing to be fully awake and alert. John's reference occurred six hours later, when Jesus needed a mild vinegar-wine to moisten his lips and make possible his final words from the cross. Knowing the objects in question clears up the confusion.

Second, study *social customs.* Rites or practices that society observed in biblical times can be crucial to understanding the biblical text. For example, Jesus' words to the Samaritan woman at Sychar shocked even her: "You are a Jew and I am a Samaritan woman. How can you ask me for a drink?" (John 4:9). Her question makes sense when we learn that Jews hated Samaritans, and that Jewish rabbis would typically refuse to speak to a woman in public. Jesus broke with this popular prejudice in winning the woman to himself. Often we must do the same today.

Third, investigate *historical facts.* Basic facts of everyday life are often presupposed by the writer but unknown to readers today. For example, Jesus' parable in Luke 11 describes a man whose friend awakens him at midnight to ask bread for a guest who has just come. The man is frustrated: "Don't bother me. The door is already locked, and my children are with me in bed. I can't get up and give you anything" (Luke 11:7).

Every detail of the story made sense to Jesus' hearers. Typical homes in his culture were one room. The back one-third was an elevated wooden platform where the family slept. The front two-thirds was a dirt floor where the animals were kept for the night. The door was locked only when the residents were asleep and wished not to be disturbed. The man without bread had committed a major social mistake, since keeping bread for hospitality was a sacred responsibility in their culture.

He made his problem his neighbor's. His pounding on the locked door would awaken the family and animals, ensuring that none slept again that night. Nonetheless, the man got up and gave his neighbor the bread he needed. Here is Jesus' point: if the man would answer such a request, how much more will God answer our prayers. Knowing the historical culture makes the parable live again.

As you investigate historical context, be especially alert to changes between the first century and ours. For instance, calling someone a "Good Samaritan" today is a compliment. In Jesus' day, the term was an oxymoron. For a Samaritan to help a wounded Jew after the Jewish priest and Levite had refused him would be akin to a black man in the 1960s helping an injured white man after the white man's pastor and deacon chairman left him for dead. When we understand and communicate the historical situation behind the text, its meaning is still as relevant as when the biblical writers first recorded it.

So, when you are familiar with the author's purpose for his book and the particular text you're studying, when you know the meaning of the author's words and phrases, and when you understand the historical and social background of the passage, then you are ready to interpret the text theologically and practically. You have laid an excellent foundation for the application of God's word to your life today.

Theological Principles

The third part of our fourfold approach deals with theological principles intended by the passage. Here it is important to consider two topics.

Scripture interprets Scripture

Now that you have developed the grammatical-historical meaning of the text, relate this meaning to the rest of God's word. Use a topical Bible or concordance to find other passages on the subject. But be careful. Never take any other passage out of its context to make it fit your study. Only relate those texts that are intended by their author for this application.

I teach a Men's Bible Study at our church on Tuesday and Thursday mornings. We were discussing James 3 and the warning against sins of speech. One of the men asked, "Which kinds of speech does he mean?" James doesn't specify. But I had looked for other Scriptures on the subject, and I had listed them in my notes: lies (Exodus 20:16); false appearances (Psalm 62:4); withholding the truth (Leviticus 5:1); and slander (Ephesians 4:31; Titus 3:1–2; 1 Peter 2:1). God's word is its own best commentary, and these references made the passage in James more specific and relevant.

General theological concepts

Now you are ready to look for intended theological principles within the passage and larger word of God. See what the text has to say about:

- God
- Humanity
- Creation and the world
- Sin
- Salvation
- Missions
- The future

What other theological significance is found within the text? What key theological contributions does the passage make to our lives today?

Let's say you're studying Romans 12:1–2:

Therefore, I urge you, brothers, in view of God's mercy, to offer your bodies as living sacrifices, holy and pleasing to God—this is your spiritual act of worship. Do not conform any longer to the pattern of this world, but be transformed by the renewing of your mind. Then you will be able to test and approve what God's will is—his good, pleasing and perfect will.

What is "therefore" there for? It takes us back to the mercies of God for which Paul expressed gratitude in Romans 11:33–36. In light of all God has done for us, this is what we are to do in response: "offer your bodies as living sacrifices." In the Greek culture of the first century, the body and the spirit were separated. The spiritual is good, the physical demeaning. In that culture's view, the point of life is to free the soul from its physical prison.

Now Paul calls us to offer our "bodies" to God, our entire lives. Not just Sunday but Monday. Not just our salvation but our service. Not just our religion but the rest of our lives, money, abilities, and opportunities. Knowing the theological context of Paul's statement helps us understand its application to our lives.

Asking theological questions brings the text into relevance. What did Paul say about God? That God loves and wants us. What did Paul say about ourselves? We can and should give ourselves fully to him. What did Paul say about this world? That we must refuse its pattern and priorities. What did Paul say about spiritual growth? That we must be transformed daily as we make our minds new in God's presence. What did Paul say about God's will? That it is good, pleasing, and perfect, but available most fully to those who are most fully his.

The theological principles discovered in a biblical text are especially important to the passage's relevance today. However, these principles must be grounded in the author's intended meaning, as discovered by grammatical-historical study. That is why our fourfold method builds theological application upon textual investigation. We should never reverse the order.

Practical Principles

The last area in our fourfold approach deals with practical applications of the text. Since human nature does not change, the Bible is always relevant and applies personally and practically to our lives.

The Scriptures were given to us to help us find and follow Jesus. If we do not seek the practical applications of the text, we have not completed its study and interpretation. Our objective should be to reproduce the original meaning of the text in today's culture.

Consider these five steps to take in applying the Bible practically.

One, write out the intended meaning of the text. On the basis of your grammatical-historical study, define the meaning and purpose of the passage for its author and original readers.

Two, note differences in setting and context. In your historical investigation, you will have observed changes in culture and context from the text to our day, some of which will significantly affect its contemporary application.

Three, make direct applications where intended by the author. Where the writer's intended meaning and purpose transfers directly to our culture and needs, make this application as practically as possible. For instance, Paul's call to "offer your bodies as living sacrifices" calls us to complete surrender and obedience. Is a part of your life not on the altar? Make this practical and personal application of the passage.

Four, seek principles in the passage when the text does not apply directly to our day. Sometimes we will study an Old Testament passage not renewed in the New Testament (such as a dietary code), or a historical event that does not prescribe a specific application (such as the Battle of Jericho, Joshua 6). In this case, do not apply the text as directly as if it were prescriptive.

Instead, seek principles in the text that might apply to today's situation and needs, keeping these principles consistent with the author's intended meaning. Dietary laws reveal the practical principle that God cares deeply about our bodies and health. The Battle of Jericho shows us that God's will, when obeyed, always leads to the victory that is his will and intention for our lives. Find such general principles within the author's intended purpose, and apply them practically.

The use of principles is often the best way to approach culture-bound biblical statements. For example, "Greet one another with a holy kiss" is a common command in Paul's letters (Romans 16:16; 1 Corinthians 16:20; 2 Corinthians 13:12; see 1 Thessalonians 5:26). The meaning of the words and grammar is just as Paul indicated.

But in Paul's society, unlike ours, people often greeted each other publicly with a kiss. In our context, these verses suggest the principle that Christians should greet each other with great kindness and love, whether this is by word, hand, or other physical expression. We are commanded to obey the principle of the text.

In the same way, commands to individuals in Scripture are not always commands to us today. Abraham was commanded to offer Isaac on the altar (Genesis 22). This prescription is not incumbent on fathers today. We need to apply the principle of the text—as a parent, I must dedicate even my children to God and his will.

Last, define at least one action that the text suggests today. When you have finished your study of the text, you should be able to describe at least one practical action you will take as a result of the author's intended purpose. Then you can determine ways to communicate this application to others.

Conclusion

The principles we have discussed in this chapter apply to every part of God's word. As we use them, we discover the meaning and application of Scripture in a way that brings its truth to life. Then we can say with the writer of Hebrews, "For the word of God is living and active. Sharper than any double-edged sword, it penetrates even to dividing soul and spirit, joints and marrow; it judges the thoughts and attitudes of the heart" (Hebrews 4:12).

We don't break the word of God; we break ourselves on it. When last did the truth of Scripture change your life?

The Bible—you truly can believe it. Let it change your life.

Notes

Chapter One Notes

1. Article I, *The Baptist Faith and Message*, 1963.
2. All references to *The Baptist Faith and Message* are to the 1963 edition.
3. Unless otherwise indicated, all Scripture quotations in this book are from The Holy Bible, New International Version (North American Edition), copyright ©1973, 1978, 1984 by the International Bible Society. Used by permission of Zondervan Publishing House.
4. Walter B. Shurden, *The Baptist Identity: Four Fragile Freedoms* (Macon, Georgia: Smyth & Helwys Publishing, Inc., 1993), 11–20.
5. Preamble, *The Baptist Faith and Message*, 1963. Quoted from the 1925 statement.
6. Quoted in Shurden, *The Baptist Identity: Four Fragile Freedoms*, 15–16, citing W. J. McGlothlin, *Baptist Confessions of Faith* (Valley Forge: Judson Press, 1911).
7. Shurden, *The Baptist Identity: Four Fragile Freedoms*, 16.
8. Shurden, *The Baptist Identity: Four Fragile Freedoms*, 18, citing William Bullein Johnson, *The Gospel Developed Through The Government and Order of the Churches of Jesus Christ* (Richmond: H. K. Ellyson, 1846), 16.
9. Shurden, *The Baptist Identity: Four Fragile Freedoms*, 18, citing G. Keith Parker, *Baptists in Europe: History and Confessions of Faith* (Nashville: Broadman Press, 1982), 280.
10. Hugh Wamble, "Baptists, the Bible, and Authority," *Proclaiming the Baptist Vision: The Bible*, ed. Walter B. Shurden (Macon, Georgia: Smyth & Helwys Publishing, Inc., 1994), 139–161.
11. Article I, *The Baptist Faith and Message*, 1963.
12. Wamble in Shurden, *Proclaiming the Baptist Vision: The Bible*, 152–153.
13. Wamble in Shurden, *Proclaiming the Baptist Vision: The Bible*, 153.
14. Wamble in Shurden, *Proclaiming the Baptist Vision: The Bible*, 153.
15. Wamble in Shurden, *Proclaiming the Baptist Vision: The Bible*, 154.
16. Wamble in Shurden, *Proclaiming the Baptist Vision: The Bible*, 154.
17. Wamble in Shurden, *Proclaiming the Baptist Vision: The Bible*, 154–155.
18. Wamble in Shurden, *Proclaiming the Baptist Vision: The Bible*, 154.

19. Edgar Young Mullins, *The Christian Religion In Its Doctrinal Expression* (Nashville: Sunday School Board of the Southern Baptist Convention, 1941 [1917]), 153.
20. W. T. Conner, *Christian Doctrine* (Nashville: Broadman and Holman, 1937), 41-42.
21. Millard J. Erickson, *Christian Theology* (Grand Rapids: Baker, 1994), 257.
22. Stanley Grenz, *Theology for the Community of God* (Nashville: Broadman and Holman, 1994), 22.
23. Russell H. Dilday, Jr., *The Doctrine of Biblical Authority* (Nashville: Convention Press, 1982), 12.

Chapter Two Notes

1. Cyprian, *On the Unity of the Church*, chapter 6.
2. Thomas, *Summa Theologiae* 1.Q1.8.
3. Thomas did allow for allegorical (spiritualizing) in interpreting the Bible, but only when these principles were grounded in the intended meaning of the biblical author, as follows: "That first meaning whereby words signify things belongs to the first sense the historical or literal. That meaning whereby things signified by words have themselves also a meaning is called the spiritual sense, which is based on the literal, and presupposes it" (*Summa* 1.Q1.10).
4. *The First Epistle of Clement* 12 (*Ante-Nicene Fathers* 1:8).
5. Justin, *Dialogue with Trypho* 42 (*Ante-Nicene Fathers* 1:215-6).
6. Clement of Alexandria, *The Instructor* II:4 (*Ante-Nicene Fathers* 2:248).
7. Origen's *Commentary on John*, X:18 (*Ante-Nicene Fathers* 10:396-9).
8. John P. Newport and William Cannon, *Why Christians Fight Over the Bible* (Nashville: Thomas Nelson, Inc., 1974), 163-164.
9. Martin Luther, *Luther's Works*, ed. Helmut T. Lehmann (Philadelphia: Fortress Press, 1967), 37:76.
10. *Letters of Martin Luther*, trans. and ed. Margaret A. Currie (London: Macmillan & Co., Ltd., 1908), 93; *Table Talk*, trans. and ed. Theodore G. Tappert (Philadelphia: Fortress Press, 1967), 346-347.
11. *Institutes* I.vi.1.
12. *Institutes* I.vi.2.

Chapter Three Notes

1. See also Craig Blomberg, *The Historical Reliability of the* Gospels (Downers Grove, Illinois: InterVarsity Press, 1987), 193.

Chapter Four Notes

1. Dan Brown, *The Da Vinci Code* (New York: Doubleday, 2003), 231 (italics his).
2. Brown, 1.
3. William Barclay, *A Spiritual Autobiography* (Grand Rapids, Michigan: Eerdmans, 1975), 90.
4. See "Text, NT," *The Interpreter's Dictionary of the Bible* (New York: Abingdon Press, 1962), 4:595.
5. This section follows closely the authoritative work of Bruce M. Metzger, *The Text of the New Testament: Its Transmission, Corruption, and Restoration*, 3d. ed. (New York: Oxford University Press, 1992), 186–206.
6. Ernst Wurthwein, *The Text of the Old Testament*, 4th ed., trans. Erroll F. Rhodes (Grand Rapids, Michigan: Eerdmans, 1992 [1979]), 116–119.
7. Metzger, 207–246.
8. The Latin for Estienne's last name is Stephanus, by which he sometimes is also known.
9. "Text, NT," *The Interpreter's Dictionary of the Bible*, 4:600–601.
10. Metzger, *The Text of the New Testament*, 224.
11. See Metzger, *A Textual Commentary on the Greek New Testament*, 2d ed. (New York: United Bible Societies, 2002), 102–106.
12. F. F. Bruce, *The New Testament Documents: Are They Reliable?* 5th rev. ed. (Downers Grove, Illinois: InterVarsity Press, 1977 [revised 1960; original 1943]), 19–20.
13. Frederic Kenyon, *The Bible and Archaeology* (New York: Harper and Brothers, 1940), 288–289; quoted by Bruce, *New Testament Documents*, 20. Italics in quoted text.
14. Brown, 231.

Chapter Five Notes

1. James Allan Francis, "One Solitary Life."
2. Sources: James D. G. Dunn, *The Evidence for Jesus* (Louisville, Kentucky: The Westminster Press, 1985); R. T. France, *The Evidence for Jesus* (Downers Grove, Illinois: InterVarsity, 1986); Gary R. Habermas, *The Verdict of History: Conclusive Evidence for the Life of Jesus* (Nashville: Thomas Nelson, 1988).
3. France, *Evidence*, 24.
4. Pliny the Younger, *Letters* 10.96–97.
5. Sources include Jeffrey L. Sheler, *Is the Bible True?* (New York: HarperSanFrancisco, 1999); and John Arthur Thompson, ed., *The Bible and Archaeology*, rev. (Grand Rapids, Michigan: Eerdmans, 1982 [original edition 1972]).

6. Sheler, *Is the Bible True?*, 59–62.
7. Sheler, *Is the Bible True?*, 101.
8. Thompson, *The Bible and Archaeology* (1972), 149.
9. Thompson, *The Bible and Archaeology* (1972), 157–161.
10. Thompson, *The Bible and Archaeology* (1972), 380.
11. Thompson, *The Bible and Archaeology* (1972), 286.
12. Sheler, *Is the Bible True?*, 110–111.
13. Thompson, *The Bible and Archaeology* (1972), 396.
14. Thompson, *The Bible and Archaeology* (1972), 399.
15. This discussion follows the treatment by Josh McDowell, *The New Evidence that Demands a Verdict* (Nashville: Thomas Nelson, 1999), 167–194. McDowell's discussion is helpful in that it depends heavily on Jewish interpretation of the Old Testament sources cited.

Chapter Six Notes

1. F. F. Bruce, *The Canon of Scripture* (Downers Grove, Illinois: InterVarsity, 1988), 17.
2. Dan Brown, *The Da Vinci Code* (New York: Doubleday, 2003), 234 (italics in original).
3. *Flavius Josephus Against Apion* 1:8. Josephus's arrangement is different from the more common twenty-four, but it includes all the books of the Hebrew Bible. In *Josephus: Complete Works*, trans. William Whiston (Grand Rapids, Michigan: Kregel Publications, 1978 [1960]).
4. *The First Apology of Justin*, ch. 67, in *The Ante-Nicene Fathers*, ed. Alexander Roberts and James Donaldson, rev. A. Cleveland Coxe, 1:186 (Grand Rapids, Michigan: Eerdmans, repr. 1989).
5. Papias, *Fragments of the Exposition of the Oracles of the Lord*, VI.
6. See "Canon of the New Testament," *The Interpreter's Dictionary of the Bible* (Nashville, Tennessee: Abingdon Press, 1976), Supplement, and "Canon of the New Testament, *The Interpreter's Dictionary of the Bible* (New York: Abingdon Press, 1962), vol. I.
7. Athanasius, *A Select Library of Nicene and Post-Nicene Fathers of the Christian Church* (Grand Rapids, Michigan: Eerdmans, repr. 1991), 4:552.
8. F. F. Bruce, *The New Testament Documents: Are They Reliable?* 5th ed. (Downers Grove, Illinois: InterVarsity, 1977), 27.
9. William Barclay, *The Making of the Bible* (London: Lutterworth Press, 1961), 10.
10. Barclay, *The Making of the Bible*, 10.

Chapter Seven Notes

1. Thomas Jefferson, *The Jefferson Bible* (Boston: Beacon Press, 1989), 5.
2. Jefferson, 11.
3. Jefferson, 30.
4. Jefferson, 147.
5. C. S. Lewis, *Miracles: A Preliminary Study* (New York: Macmillan, 1947), 10.
6. Lewis, *Miracles*, 10.
7. Norman Geisler and Ron Brooks, *When Skeptics Ask: A Handbook of Christian Evidences* (Wheaton, Illinois: Victor Books, 1990), 88.
8. Colin Brown, *Miracles and the Critical Mind* (Grand Rapids, Michigan: Eerdmans, 1984), 4. Brown's defense of miracles stands with C. S. Lewis's *Miracles* as perhaps the finest on our subject available today.
9. Antony Flew, "Theology and Falsification" in *The Existence of God*, ed. John Hick (New York: Macmillan, 1964), 224–228.
10. See David Hume, *An Enquiry Concerning Human Understanding* (LaSalle, Illinois: Open Court, 1966 [1907]), 128–129.
11. Rudolf Bultmann, "New Testament and Mythology," in *Kerygma and Myth*, ed. Hans Werner Bartsch (New York: Harper and Row, 1961), 4.
12. T. F. Torrance, "The Church in the New Era of Scientific and Cosmological Change," *Theology in Reconstruction* (Grand Rapids: Eerdmans, 1975), 270. See also his *Preaching Christ Today: The Gospel and Scientific Thinking* (Grand Rapids: Eerdmans, 1994), 61–63.
13. Albert Einstein, quoted by Stanley L. Jaki, "Theological Aspects of Creative Science," *Creation, Christ and Culture—Studies in Honor of T. F. Torrance*, ed. Richard W. A. McKinney (Edinburgh: T. & T. Clark, 1976), 164.
14. Cited in Brown, *Miracles of the Modern Mind*, 57–58.
15. Cited in Brown, *Miracles of the Modern Mind*, 183–188.
16. J. B. Phillips, *Your God Is Too Small* (New York: Macmillan, 1972 [1961]), 123–124 (italics in original).

Chapter Eight Notes

1. *Discourse on Method*, part 4.
2. *Essay Concerning Human Understanding* II.1.2.
3. See *An Enquire Concerning Human Understanding* (La Salle, Illinois: Open Court, 1967), 49, 84.
4. See *Prolegomena to Any Future Metaphysics* (Indianapolis, Indiana: The Library of Liberal Arts, 1950 [1783]), 5–12.

5. See *Groundwork of the Metaphysics of Morals*, trans. H. J. Paton (New York: Harper Torchbooks, 1967), 126–127.
6. Stanley Grenz, *A Primer on Postmodernism* (Grand Rapids: Eerdmans, 1986), 88.
7. See Friedrich Nietzsche, *The Genealogy of Morals*, trans. F. Golffing (Garden City, NY: Doubleday, 1956), 255; 209–10; *Beyond Good and Evil*, trans. M. Cowan (Chicago: Henry Regnery, 1955), 18–19, 100–101.
8. Friedrich Schleiermacher, *The Christian Faith*, ed. H. R. Mackintosh and J. S. Stewart (Edinburgh: T. & T. Clark, 1976), 131.
9. Philosophers and other scholars who have written in this area include Wilhelm Dithey (1833–1911); Hans-Georg Gadamer (1900–2002); Ludwig Wittgenstein (1899–1951); Michel Foncal (1926–84); Jaques Derrida (born 1930); and Richard Roty (born 1931).

Chapter Nine Notes

1. Clark Pinnock, *The Scripture Principle* (San Francisco: Harper and Row, 1984), 78.
2. Robert Preus, "The Inerrancy of Scripture," *The Proceedings of the Conference on Biblical Inerrancy 1987* (Nashville: Broadman Press), 49.
3. Preus, 49.
4. "Chicago Statement on Biblical Inerrancy," Exposition C: Infallibility, Inerrancy, Interpretation.
5. *Dei Verbum*, ch. III, art. 11.
6. Robert J. Coleman, "Reconsidering 'Limited Inerrancy,'' in *Evangelicals and Inerrancy*, ed. Ronald Youngblood (Nashville: Thomas Nelson, 1984), 165–166.
7. Coleman, 166–167.
8. See Rex A. Koivisto, "Stephen's Speech: A Case Study in Rhetorical and Biblical Inerrancy," in *Evangelicals and Inerrancy*, 217–229.
9. Pinnock, 78.
10. Preus, 51–55.
11. "Chicago Statement on Biblical Inerrancy," Exposition E: Transmission and Translation.
12. See *The Battle for the Bible* (Grand Rapids, Michigan: Zondervan, 1976) and "An Historian Looks at Inerrancy," in *Evangelicals and Inerrancy*, 49–58.
13. "An Historian," *Evangelicals and Inerrancy*, 49.
14. Origen's *Commentary on John*, X:18 (*Ante-Nicene Fathers* 10:396–9).
15. Augustine, Sermon 81, *Sermons on New Testament Lessons, Nicene and Post-Nicene Fathers*, first series, 6:503. See also Augustine, *Quaestiones Evangeliorum*, II, 19, cited in C.H. Dodd, *The Parables of the Kingdom*, rev. (New York: Charles Scribner's Sons, 1961), 1–2.

16. Jack B. Rogers and Donald K. McKim, *The Authority and Interpretation of the Bible: An Historical Approach* (New York: Harper and Row, 1979), xvii-xviii, 172–188.
17. Mark Noll, "A Brief History of Inerrancy, Mostly in America," in *Proceedings,* 17–19.
18. Edwin Yamauchi, "taher," *Theological Dictionary of the Old Testament*, ed. R. Laird Harris (Chicago: Moody Press, 1980), 1:343; hereafter abbreviated *TDOT.*
19. John E. Hartley, "sarap," *TDOT*, 2:778.
20. J. Barton Payne, "tamam," *TDOT*, 2:973-974.
21. Jack B. Scott, "aman," *TDOT*, 1:51–53.
22. Fritz Rienecker, *A Linguistic Key to the Greek New Testament*, trans. and rev. Cleon L. Rogers, Jr. (Grand Rapids: Zondervan, 1976), 1:243.
23. A. T. Robertson, *Word Pictures in the New Testament* (Nashville, Tennessee: Broadman Press, 1932), V:279.
24. Gottleib Schrenk, "heiros," *TDNT*, 3:222–223.

Chapter Ten Notes

1. The discussion in this chapter is a revision and enlargement of my earlier study of general hermeneutics in *Seven Crucial Questions about the Bible* (Nashville: Broadman and Holman, 1994), 138–163. Other sources include A. Berkeley Michelson, *Interpreting the Bible* (Grand Rapids: Eerdmans, 1989 [1963]); Bernard Ramm, *Protestant Biblical Interpretation*, 3d. rev. ed. (Grand Rapids: Baker, 1971); Walter Henrichsen and Gayle Jackson, *Studying, Interpreting, and Applying the Bible* (Grand Rapids: Lamplighter Books, Zondervan, 1990); and Gordon D. Fee and Douglas Stuart, *How to Read the Bible for All Its Worth*, 2d. ed. (Grand Rapids: Zondervan, 1993).
2. Fritz Rienecker, *A Linguistic Key to the Greek New Testament*, trans. and rev. Cleon L. Rogers, Jr. (Grand Rapids, Michigan: Zondervan, 1980), 2:281.
3. Article I, *The Baptist Faith and Message*, 1963.
4. Robert Frost, "The Road Not Taken."

Chapter Eleven Notes

1. As in the previous chapter, this discussion is an enlargement of my previous description of general hermeneutics in *Seven Crucial Questions About the Bible* (Nashville: Broadman and Holman, 1994).
2. See also chapter 3, page 37, of *The Bible—You Can Believe It.*

How to Order More Bible Study Materials

It's easy! Just fill in the following information. For additional Bible study materials, see www.baptistwaypress.org or get a complete order form of available materials by calling 1-866-249-1799 or e-mailing baptistway@bgct.org.

Title of item	Price	Quantity	Cost
This Study:			
The Bible—You Can Believe It	$4.95	________	________
The Bible—You Can Believe It: Teaching Guide	$1.95	________	________
Bible Studies:			
Genesis 12—50: Family Matters—Study Guide	$1.95	________	________
Genesis 12—50: Family Matters—Large Print Study Guide	$1.95	________	________
Genesis 12—50: Family Matters—Teaching Guide	$2.45	________	________
Exodus: Freed to Follow God —Study Guide	$2.35	________	________
Exodus: Freed to Follow God —Large Print Study Guide	$2.35	________	________
Exodus: Freed to Follow God —Teaching Guide	$2.95	________	________
Leviticus, Numbers, Deuteronomy—Study Guide	$2.35	________	________
Leviticus, Numbers, Deuteronomy—Large Print Study Guide	$2.35	________	________
Leviticus, Numbers, Deuteronomy—Teaching Guide	$2.95	________	________
Joshua, Judges—Study Guide	$2.35	________	________
Joshua, Judges—Large Print Study Guide	$2.35	________	________
Joshua, Judges—Teaching Guide	$2.95	________	________
Isaiah and Jeremiah—Study Guide	$1.95	________	________
Isaiah and Jeremiah—Teaching Guide	$2.45	________	________
Amos, Hosea, Micah—Study Guide	$1.95	________	________
Amos, Hosea, Micah—Teaching Guide	$2.45	________	________
Matthew: Jesus' Teachings—Study Guide	$2.35	________	________
Matthew: Jesus' Teachings—Large Print Study Guide	$2.35	________	________
Matthew: Jesus' Teachings—Teaching Guide	$2.95	________	________
Jesus in the Gospel of Mark—Study Guide	$1.95	________	________
Jesus in the Gospel of Mark—Large Print Study Guide	$1.95	________	________
Jesus in the Gospel of Mark—Teaching Guide	$2.45	________	________
Luke: Journeying to the Cross—Study Guide	$2.35	________	________
Luke: Journeying to the Cross—Large Print Study Guide	$2.35	________	________
Luke: Journeying to the Cross —Teaching Guide	$2.95	________	________
1 Corinthians—Study Guide	$1.95	________	________
1 Corinthians—Large Print Study Guide	$1.95	________	________
1 Corinthians—Teaching Guide	$2.45	________	________
2 Corinthians: Taking Ministry Personally—Study Guide	$2.35	________	________
2 Corinthians: Taking Ministry Personally—Large Print Study Guide	$2.35	________	________
2 Corinthians: Taking Ministry Personally —Teaching Guide	$2.95	________	________
Hebrews and James—Study Guide	$1.95	________	________
Hebrews and James—Large Print Study Guide	$1.95	________	________
Hebrews and James—Teaching Guide	$2.45	________	________
Letters of John and Peter—Study Guide	$1.95	________	________
Letters of John and Peter—Large Print Study Guide	$1.95	________	________
Letters of John and Peter—Teaching Guide	$2.45	________	________
Revelation—Study Guide	$2.35	________	________
Revelation—Large Print Study Guide	$2.35	________	________
Revelation—Teaching Guide	$2.95	________	________

Beliefs Important to Baptists

Beliefs Important to Baptists—Study Guide (one-volume edition; includes all lessons)	$2.35	______	______
Beliefs Important to Baptists—Teaching Guide (one-volume edition; includes all lessons)	$1.95	______	______
Who in the World Are Baptists, Anyway? (one lesson)	$ .45	______	______
Who in the World Are Baptists, Anyway?—Teacher's Edition	$ .55	______	______
Beliefs Important to Baptists: I (four lessons)	$1.35	______	______
Beliefs Important to Baptists: I—Teacher's Edition	$1.75	______	______
Beliefs Important to Baptists: II (four lessons)	$1.35	______	______
Beliefs Important to Baptists: II—Teacher's Edition	$1.75	______	______
Beliefs Important to Baptists: III (four lessons)	$1.35	______	______
Beliefs Important to Baptists: III—Teacher's Edition	$1.75	______	______

For Children

Let's Explore Baptist Beliefs	$3.95	______	______
Let's Explore Baptist Beliefs—Leader's Guide	$2.95	______	______

Subtotal	______
Standard Shipping*	
Basic Charge	$6.00
Plus 12% of Subtotal	______
TOTAL	______

*Please allow three weeks for standard delivery. For express shipping service: Call 1-866-249-1799 for information on additional charges.

____
YOUR NAME PHONE

____
YOUR CHURCH DATE ORDERED

____
MAILING ADDRESS

____
CITY STATE ZIP CODE

MAIL this form with your check for the total amount to
BAPTISTWAY PRESS, Baptist General Convention of Texas,
333 North Washington, Dallas, TX 75246-1798
(Make checks to "Baptist Executive Board.")

OR, **FAX** your order anytime to: 214-828-5187, and we will bill you.

OR, **CALL** your order toll-free: 1-866-249-1799 (8:30 a.m.-5:00 p.m., M-F), and we will bill you.

OR, **E-MAIL** your order to our internet e-mail address: baptistway@bgct.org, and we will bill you.

OR, **ORDER ONLINE** at www.baptistwaypress.org.

We look forward to receiving your order! Thank you!